A Good **Foundation**
and a **Fulfilled**
Life

A GOOD FOUNDATION AND A FULFILLED LIFE

Published by Chaplain Publishing
3104 County Road 7520
Lubbock, TX 79423
www.chaplainpublishing.com

ISBN: 978-1-941549-46-9

Cover and text design: NiTROhype Creative
www.nitrohype.com

Printed in the United States of America

A Good Foundation and a Fulfilled Life

Ron Fulenwider

Table of Contents

A Tribute to Bruce D. Fulenwider

"My Hero"
1938-2019

My brother grew up in Southern Illinois in the 1940s and 1950s. He was three years older than me and was always my protector, especially in high school. Bruce was very popular his entire life. Recently I talked with two of my brother's good friends Gary Meyer and Dale Brooks and both said that Bruce was well liked and always willing to help where needed. I remember another good friend Richard Chamness saying years later that Bruce was like a father to him. Richard, when traveling to Texas, would always make a special trip to Huntsville to visit with Bruce.

Bruce passed away March 27, 2019, at his home in Huntsville, Texas. He had just turned 81 in February. He moved with his family to Huntsville in 1968. He started his career working for Champion Paper Company and then working at Sam Houston State University as the Head Landscaper for the University for 25 years before retiring. He had 100 men working under his management and 10 greenhouses. The Sam Houston landscape reminded me so much of Southern Illinois University's landscape. It was one of the most beautiful campuses I have ever visited.

Growing up both Bruce and I had the unique opportunity to work side by side with our parents. When reading this book, I hope you will enjoy all the funny stories of the many goofy things both Bruce and I did. We were often called gourd heads. It is unfortunate that farm jobs have been replaced with jobs in cities and towns because that takes away the chance to work alongside parents like Bruce and I did.

Bruce proudly served in the United States Navy from 1956-1960.

Bruce loved the outdoors. He was an avid hunter and fisherman, taking after our father Jean D. Fulenwider. He spent hours in his garden, which he found very relaxing. He never met a stranger and was loved by everyone that knew him. His neighbors joked that he was mayor of Eucalyptus Road, the road on which he lived and which he and his wife named.

Bruce was a member of the Northside Baptist Church in Huntsville. His minister, Reagan Cooksey, a good friend, proceeded over the memorial service. He told of the many good times he and Bruce had while hunting and fishing.

Bruce was the landscaper for Northside Baptist Church. After working at the church, he later became an active member. He was strong in his faith and his love for Christ. As a result, he was strong near the end of his life. He told me he was ready to be with Christ, and this made it so much better for all of us. I remember him saying in one of his hospital stays that a roommate was crying and saying he didn't want to die. Bruce said, "I don't want to die, but my faith makes it easier to deal with."

I hope you readers will enjoy the many funny and sometimes crazy things Bruce and I did growing up in Southern Illinois and Little Egypt during the '40s, '50s, and '60s.

Chapter 1
The Early Years

GROWING UP ON THE FAMILY FARM

I was born June 14th, 1941, in Anna, Illinois, in the old Willard Memorial Hospital. The current Anna-Jonesboro High School gymnasium stands in almost the exact same spot.

When I was five weeks old, Mom and Dad moved from a small farm off of Ashlar Drive in Jonesboro to an 80-acre farm 3 1/2 miles southwest of Jonesboro. The farm had been in the family for many years. This is where my great grandpa, my grandpa, and my dad grew up. It was called Lake Hill. Why? I don't know, because there isn't a lake anywhere.

On this land was a little one-room school called Lake Hill School. In earlier years, it was known as the Fulenwider School. I know that the school had a lot of Fulenwider kids. My grandpa had ten children just in the Lake Hill school area, which was no larger than 80 acres. The State of Illinois had over 12,000 school districts. In the Union County area there were dozens of school districts. Just off the old Cape Road, now called the Trail of Tears Road, there were many schools. Lake Hill, Meisenheimer, Lingle Center Hill, Miller, and Lyerla were all located within a five-mile radius. My Aunt Zada Foehr taught at the Lyerla one-room school. Teachers during those years taught at many different schools over their careers. I know of three schools where my aunt taught - Lyerla, Jonesboro, and Sitter. The salaries would be $700 or $800 per year. The school years in many districts would only last eight months. Many schools would let students out during May for them to work on the farm. Many students would pick strawberries during mid-to-late May. Today, most schools are in session for nine months.

The Lake Hill School closed in 1943, so I missed getting to go to a one-room by five years. It was fascinating to go into the school and see the old wooden desks, the slate chalkboards, the cloakroom, and to ring the old bell that brought many of my aunts and dad to school. The old bell is still in use in my yard. My grandchildren like to ring the bell. It is a #25 yoke bell and still has an enormous ring to it.

LIFE ON THE FARM

Life on the farm in the '40s and '50s could be lonesome at times because we didn't go to town on a daily basis, especially during the spring and summer months. We had plenty of food that we grew or raised on the farm. I know this sounds strange to the youth growing up today;

10

it's nothing to go to town now. The world today is much smaller with internet, cell phones, and social media. We had a large garden; we raised sheep, hogs, and cattle. We milked about three cows for our milk consumption.

We had hog-killing days, and we processed our own meat products. We didn't have electricity until 1952, so our meats and other food items were taken to the Union County Locker plant located on Davie Street in Anna, Illinois. What was not frozen or processed, Mom would can. She put up hundreds of quarts of blackberries, peaches, and other fruits and vegetables.

We had some obstacles to overcome. I remember going blackberry picking numerous times, carrying a gallon bucket. We had a few hazards to watch out for, especially Timber rattlesnakes and copperheads. Oblivious to any hazards, I would begin my berry-picking journey in short pants, without any knife and, of course, no cell phone. I look back and see how naïve I was. Believe it or not, my parents didn't think much about me journeying out that way either. At least I don't remember them saying anything—possibly selective hearing. God was with me on all of those picking days.

We killed five or six copperheads and rattlers annually. Most were killed while combining or mowing hay. We were three and one-half miles from a doctor. I often wonder what would have happened if I had been bitten by a copperhead snake. The venom is much more deadly than a rattlesnake. What if I had passed out from excitement, or Dad had the car and Mom couldn't take me to our family doctor? God is good! It wasn't my time!

The food we consumed was grown mostly organically. Our garden was about one-half acre. It was vital, as food from the grocer was expensive for a family making less than $2,000 a year. Anything grown in the garden was a saving for our family. We all worked in the garden during our leisure time. We would purchase basic condiments at the grocer. That would save the family money, especially during the times when our farming production was low. The cost of growing a garden was much cheaper, and organic foods were so much healthier.

The most expensive item in gardening would be the fertilizer. We did use some chemicals, but we would watch for insects and pick them off of the plants. We didn't have many problems with plant disease at that time. Our main organic fertilizer was cow and sheep manure.

WEEKENDS

Saturdays and Sundays were important times for social events. We used to gather with our close neighbor friends, have hamburger cookout dinners, and make homemade ice cream. If you've never had homemade ice cream cranked by hand, you have missed a treat. We would add home-grown peaches or some other locally grown fruit to enhance the flavor that much more. After the ice cream was cranked to where it couldn't be cranked anymore, we would then pack the top of the ice cream freezer with blankets or some other type of covering and let the ice cream set another thirty minutes until it was totally frozen.

Sundays were spent with families and attending church. The rural churches were well-attended in those days. Today, many rural churches have closed their doors.

I can name many churches in Union County that are closed or are close to locking the doors. One of the main reasons is the loss of many small farms. Many farmers have left the farm to go to the city to find jobs. A farmer in the '40s and '50s could raise a family on eighty acres. As modernization entered the scene, small farms gave way to very large farms that had acreage of 1,500 to 2,000. Tractors in the 1940s and 1950s were not equipped with cabs and radios and all kinds of special accessories. The newer tractors and self-propelled combines could plant many more acres in just a few hours than could the small farmer, who, like us, was using an 8N Ford tractor, or an All-Crop AC pull-type combine. We couldn't compete, nor could we buy a thousand acres of land or expensive modern equipment. Another reason the rural churches are disappearing is that the farmer's children leave the rural area for college. After college, they find jobs that are not available in rural areas where there is very little industry.

When Bruce and I grew up on the Lake Hill farm, it was understood that you attended church. Mom taught Sunday school for over 30 years. We would sometimes fake illness so we could play. Mom saw through it. Sometimes, we just didn't want to take a bath and get ready. Sad! We still have many churches located in small towns and cities that are thriving. But the churches located out near the small farms are basically disappearing.

NEAR TRAGEDY AT AGE TWO

When I was two years of age, I almost lost my life. My father, Jean, was working near the house, perhaps 100 yards from home. He was constructing a small pond with a Cat 25 crawler tractor. I followed my dad into the area just below the house where he was working. He saw me and instructed me to go back to the house. I was curious about what he was doing, so I didn't return to the house. I wanted to get up on the tractor. Dad didn't see me, so he thought I had returned to the house, and he was preoccupied with the pond construction. As he was backing the tractor, he looked down and I was underneath the 14" track of the crawler. In his panic, he hit the brake and killed the engine. In the early '40s, most tractors didn't have starters. Dad had to get off the tractor, get the crank and start the engine, then get back up on the tractor and back it off of me. He picked me up instantly and ran as hard as could, yelling for my mom. As my mom approached, Dad was yelling, "I've killed my boy! I've killed my boy!" Mom and Dad got me to the hospital, and Dr. Roy Keith examined me and said I had a broken leg. In the early '40s,

that required a cast with a pulley to elevate the leg and a lot of bed rest.

He said that I would be ok and that I was very lucky. The crawler track missed my intestines by inches. Dr. Roy Keith was a special person that night. He brought me into the world, and he kept me in the world. God spared my life. I was too young to remember much about the ordeal. To this day, however, I still remark about the incident and believe I remember it. More probable is the fact that I heard so many people talking about it that I actually started thinking that I remembered. Two years of age is awfully young to remember anything. What saved me was muddy ground. As the track of the crawler rolled over me, my body was pushed down into the mud. Had the ground been hard, only God knows whether I would have lived or died. Dr. Keith must have done a great job, because I have never suffered any ill effects from the accident.

BASKETBALL

As mentioned earlier, we had the old one-room school called Lake Hill. In earlier years it was known as the Fulenwider School. My love for basketball started early in life. I put a basketball goal up at one end of the school so I could play basketball in the winter months. It worked well when I was pretty small, but in later years, I found the ceiling a little low for shooting with any kind of arch. That is when I developed a real passion for basketball. Mom and Dad always made sure I had a ball and a good goal so that I could practice. Kids today would laugh at the kind of ball we had. The basketball had a bladder inside the leather casing. The ball didn't always bounce accurately because of the lacing on the outside. Because of the misshaped basketball, I learned to handle it better because I didn't know which way it would bounce.

Fulenwider School, later known as Lake Hill.

When I wasn't doing chores, I would play basketball. I would play many make-believe games as I transformed that old one-room school into an NBA arena. My heroes were Dolph Schayes, Bob Pettit, and Bill Russell—all top 50 players in the history of the NBA. Pettit was a St Louis Hawk, Russell a Boston Celtic, and Schayes a Syracuse National. All three are now in their mid-to-late 80s. I hoped that I would be a good player someday. I imagined I was playing against Bob Pettit and Bill Russell all the time. I don't know that I ever thought I would play in the

NBA. I was so small in the seventh grade (4' 11"). By the time I reached high school, I was only 5' 1". I played two years of basketball at Jonesboro Grade School. Believe it or not, I played forward on the team. I was pretty quick, and I could get around the taller players and score. We played in tiny rural schools that had the double-time (center) lines. The free- throw lanes were six-feet at that time. Today, they are twelve feet.

I remember game day. We got to wear our cotton warm-up jackets. At the time we thought they were beautiful. Looking back now, they were plain ugly. They were made of cotton and not attractive like today's warm-ups. We couldn't wait to get to the Twins Cafe on the square to display our warm-ups. We did want to show off a little for the girls.

My parents permitted me to play basketball, but I would have to find a way home on some days. The custodian lived about a mile and a half from me and took me home sometimes. The other days, I would thumb home from the Jonesboro square. I lived three and a half miles from the school, which isn't that far by car, but too far to walk. Between Mom and the custodian, I would have a ride three days a week. I was very successful in thumbing home because of neighbors and people traveling south on Route 127. Practice usually lasted until 5:00 p.m., and it would already be getting dark. I remember seeing scary things at times going home. Most rides got me to within a mile of my house. Today, one wouldn't think of letting their child thumb home.

My love for basketball continued to grow. But I was so small, I didn't make the team my freshman year of high school. I kept practicing in physical education and at home on my old-school NBA court. My opportunity to play didn't come until my senior year because I had to work on the farm after school. Dad needed my help to make ends meet. Life was tough at that time financially. My senior year, I tried out and made the team. By then, I was 6'1". My coach knew that I had worked hard in physical education, and I really wanted to play my senior year. I had played a lot of FFA ball which helped me develop my fundamentals. I was able to contribute and play a reasonable amount of time. I was sixth man behind Tony Ferrell, an all-conference player who held the conference scoring record for a number of years. Tony was my close friend and teammate in grade school. We started on the Jonesboro Bulldogs together. My chance to play my most important high school game came in the Regional Tournament being held at Anna-Jonesboro in 1959. It was the regional championship against Mounds Douglas High School (now Meridian). Tony had gotten into foul trouble, and I came in for him. The game was very close, and I was a nervous wreck. I made six out of six free throws while he was on the bench. It turned out that those six free throws helped seal the victory in the championship game. We won the game 62-59 over a fine Mounds team. I try to tell my kids today you have to work hard to achieve your goals, whatever they are.

Moving forward, I enrolled at Southeast Missouri State and spent three years as an athletic trainer. My love of the game was still very much alive. My three years sitting next to the head coach was so rewarding. I absorbed everything that I could during those three years. I made every game (120) and every practice during my time at Southeast Missouri State. I met some famous coaches while at college. As the trainer and manager, I would let the coaches from the visiting schools come in for pregame practice. One such coach was Gene Bartow, who, at the time, was the Central Missouri State coach. He was a very personable man with whom I enjoyed talking. Later in his career, he replaced John Wooden at UCLA. He had worked his way up through the ranks with coaching positions at Illinois and Memphis State. He established the UAB program in Alabama. The University of Alabama at Birmingham is currently one of the premier programs in Division I basketball.

Following my college career, I was drafted into the United States Navy in 1965. I served three years. With my degree in physical education, I served part-time as an Athletic Petty Officer and played basketball for the Navy. I was selected to the Puget Sound All-Navy team in 1967 and played basketball in the All-Navy games in San Francisco. During my Navy career, I was privileged to be part of an outstanding team. The team was made up of both enlisted men and officers. We played 42 games and won 38. It was so much fun playing the different naval teams. We played many teams made up of men from all the various naval entities. Many of the teams would be from the ships docked at the Puget Sound Naval Shipyard.

I had many of my childhood dreams met. I was able to meet Bob Pettit, Oscar Robertson, and Dolph Schayes. I was privileged to meet and work with Bob Love of Chicago Bulls fame. I worked basketball camps and did motivational programs with Bob for about 17 years while working as the Health and Safety Director for the Laborers' International Union of North America. He was the guest celebrity golfer at three of our Tom Sherrill Memorial Golf Scrambles. We traveled all over the Midwest and spent a week in Hawaii and Las Vegas working together. I would have never imagined 50 years earlier that those dreams would come true. I have been so blessed! Presently, I'm in my 12th year teaching K-8 physical educational at Lick Creek Elementary. I do annual basketball and sports speed development camps with Olympic Gold Medalist Willie Smith and Olympic High Jumper Cameron Wright. This will be our 26th year to do the camps.

Chapter 2

Christmas

CHRISTMAS ON THE FARM

We had numerous red cedar evergreen trees in the wooded areas on our farm. It sounds so simple, but our time spent looking for a tree was so much fun. We looked for a beautiful deep green color and the ideal sized and shaped tree that would fit perfectly in our little bungalow. We had our axe with us, and as soon as we all agreed on the tree, off to the house we would go. Upon arrival, we would get the tree into a container and water it. I still remember that red cedar smell. Kids today would probably say, "It doesn't sound like a lot of fun to me." But things were much simpler in the '40s.

Decorating a tree was much different then, too. We didn't have electricity, so we decorated by kerosene lamp. And that meant no strings of electric lights. The tree decorations were shiny ornaments that would reflect the light from the lamps. We would pop popcorn, string it, and wrap it around the tree. We had shiny strands of tinsel to represent ice on the tree, and we used cotton for snow. It wouldn't measure up to today's standard, but that was all we had to work with. It was a wonderful family activity, and our beautiful tree helped pass the time on long December nights.

Christmas was our favorite time of year. The farm houses were all decorated; trees went up. We could look across the fields and see some of our neighbor's house lights. It was even nicer after a big snow. It really enhanced the spirit of Christmas. It seems like we had more white Christmases then than we do today. I remember several very cold and snowy Christmases. We had some very nice hillsides to sleigh ride on.

CHRISTMAS DAY

The excitement on Christmas was much like today. Kids woke up and ran to the Christmas tree just like they do today. Kids haven't changed that much as far as Christmas goes. About the only difference is the number of gifts we would receive. Bruce and I would usually get three gifts. That was fine, because that was all we expected. We usually got one game and some clothing. Checkers, Monopoly, and playing cards were popular in the '50s and '60s.

I really wanted a Lionel train and a Roy Rogers cowboy suit with a two-pistol gun holster. I got both. The Lionel train was a tough order. Dad said it was going to cost $13, and he wasn't sure if he could afford it. I persisted and finally won out. I doubt if I got a third gift that year, since the train was so expensive. I remember Bruce got a Daisy Red Ryder BB gun. We shared the gun when we could. Mom would say, "Now, be careful, and don't shoot your eye out." When the movie *A Christmas Story* came out, I remember Little Ralphie's mom saying, "Now, don't shoot your eye out." It sure brought back memories of that time in our lives. Several years, Dad would find used items in good condition. One Christmas, we got two used bicycles. We would ride our bikes everywhere, including up and down the Old Cape Road to Plank Hill and back. Several times, we rode to Mill Creek down Route I-27. Today, that would not be possible with all the traffic and security issues.

The train set and the Roy Rogers suit and guns are the greatest childhood gifts I received. That train set and Roy Rogers outfit stayed around for many years. When I grew older, we handed them down to my cousin who had them for several more years.

Two Christmases in Florida (1948 & 1952)

What a trip for two boys who hadn't been much of anywhere during the first decade of their lives! Dad had three sisters who lived in Florida, and they requested that we visit them. It seems like a trip like that would be too expensive for a farmer making only $1,800 a year. My aunt who lived in West Palm Beach made her home available to us. We would be in Florida about a week since we would have to be back in school in early January. We had never seen the ocean or been on a beach. So, the trip was going to be an exciting one. We departed for Florida in our

1948 Ford. I wish I had that car today. In the late '40s, we didn't have any Interstate Highways. So, we departed from Jonesboro traveling down Route 127 towards Cairo, Illinois. Bruce and I started asking Mom and Dad, "When are we going to get there." That was only 35 miles from home. The journey to West Palm Beach was a two-day trip. 1,100 miles in a 1948 Ford traveling on two-lane highways was an adventure. We also had to go through nearly every major city on the way. I remember going through Birmingham, Mobile, and Montgomery, Alabama; and into the panhandle of Florida. It wasn't long into the trip that Bruce and I got bored and started fighting and fussing at each other. I thought we were never going to get there.

The hilarious part of the trip was Dad trying to find the cheapest gas and least expensive motel. Gasoline in the late forties was around 18 to 20 cents a gallon. Most of the motels ran around seven or eight dollars a night. He would keep driving saying he could beat a certain-priced motel. Well, one time he kept driving until we ran out of highway. That's right, we ran out of paved highway looking for a $6.95 hotel stay. If I remember correctly, we were in Alabama. In 1948, a lot of the highway construction was not complete. One would have to watch carefully for the detour signs. Dad, however, was looking for motel prices, not detour signs. Mom said, "Jean, I told you we were going to get lost." Of course, Dad kept saying he knew where he was going.

We were about to enter the dirt road, so Dad reluctantly turned around, and we probably paid $7.95. I wish Mom and Dad were still around to tell me exactly what he did pay. Bruce and I were old enough to see the humor in all of this and have continued to enjoy the memory. I'm

24

sure Mom found no humor in the dilemma until years later.

And just think about how cheap that gasoline was. Dad would pull into a service station and tell the attendant to fill it up with Ethyl. Ethyl was the high-grade gas. In those days, all gas stations had full-service attendants. They would check the oil, wipe the windows, and pump the gas. A 20-gallon tank of gas usually ran about $3.50 to $4.00. An 1,100-mile trip would take about seven tanks of gas. We spent about $28.00 for gas on the round trip. Can you imagine that?

We ate well on the trip, too. There were many wonderful restaurants during that period of time. It was before fast food restaurants. There was no such thing as McDonald's, Hardees, Dairy Queen, or Wendy's. The prices of food at those sit-down restaurants were in line with the other prices I mentioned. We could get a complete breakfast of eggs, bacon, toast, and grits with orange juice or coffee for 65 cents. The cost for the four of us was about $3.00, including the tip. The three meals down to West Palm Beach and back totaled $18.00. There and back, the total cost of that week-long trip was less than $100, and the stay with Dad's sister and husband was probably less than $20.

Christmas in Florida seemed so strange. The daytime temperature was always in the 80s, and the skies were clear and sunny. How was Santa Claus going to arrive without snow? The evenings were chilly, however, so they did have gas fireplaces which took the chill off the rooms. We stayed most of our time with Aunt Pete and Uncle Rick. They had a daughter my age. It was so much fun going to the beach. It was a far cry from swimming in

Dutch Creek's Blue Hole area. I will never forget the thrill of going into the ocean the very first time. The waves would carry us back onto the beach. The saltwater took some getting used to. It would burn the eyes pretty good. We learned to close our eyes as much as we could. When we weren't swimming, we would build sandcastles, but we had to watch out for jellyfish. They could administer quite a sting if one wasn't careful about where they walked.

My dad's other sister, Aunt Nita, and husband Uncle Bud would come down to Aunt Pete's with our two cousins Jan and Mike. They had an outdoor skating rink in Belle Glade, FL. We played non-stop together those few days. Mike and I got this brilliant idea that we could make some money selling coconuts. Aunt Pete lived in a nice area of West Palm Beach that had quite a few palm trees. Mike was six, I was seven, and we loaded the little wagon with coconuts and went all over the neighborhood trying to sell coconuts for a dollar each. Guess what? We didn't sell one coconut. We weren't too smart trying to sell coconuts to the neighbors who had coconuts laying all over their yards.

We returned to Florida four years later with primarily the same agenda—the beach, Christmas together, fellowship with our families. One thing Mike and I didn't do was try to sell coconuts to the neighbors.

One memorable thing happened to Mom on this trip. She went fishing on the beach near West Palm Beach. A large hammerhead shark got on her line. Even though the line was heavy duty, the shark was a bit too much for Mom. She got so excited but held on tight to the rod and reel. She fought for a few minutes before Uncle Rick stepped in to help land the shark. During the struggle, we couldn't tell what was on the line. We were hoping it would be a big game fish of some kind. Mom never forgot that experience. The shark looked like it might have weighed 15 or 20 pounds. In the picture, Bruce is holding the shark. The fish I'm holding is a whopping half pound.

Chapter 3

On the Farm

Working with Mom and Dad

Bruce and I have wonderful memories of working alongside Mom and Dad. With Dad, we made hay and combined and harvested corn, beans, and wheat. We would do our own combining, and then help our neighbor harvest their crops. It was hard work, but we didn't complain that much. Dad had a large fruit farm in the late '30s and early '40s. That was before we were old enough to help. My grandfather J.L. Fulenwider had a 75-acre peach farm for several years. Dad had some very profitable years raising peaches during the war. But too many years of bad climates and low prices after WWII put him out of the peach-growing business. But Bruce and I remember the fun times with all of the workers.

Those were wonderful times working with Dad. We had some trying moments when I'm sure Dad wanted to disown us. As kids, Bruce and I were very prone to tearing up equipment. Dad would say, "You birds are going to break me." Our judgment was not very good. There wasn't a summer that went by that we didn't tear something up.

We tore the unloading auger off the combine. We would tear off the mirrors on the Dodge pickup pulling up too close to the combine while unloading the hopper. We usually took at least one mirror off the truck every summer. Breaking equipment was financially costly because of the lost time and the price of ordering replacement parts. We usually had to go to Marion or Jackson to get the parts.

We were also accused of losing tools, but we both thought Dad might have lost a few himself. But we never dared to suggest that! It was frustrating when one needed a certain tool, and it would be missing. There we'd be, out in the middle of the field in 95-degree heat, broken down, and the tool we needed was missing. Believe it or not, bailing wire saved the day more than once. Those were heated times for sure, both the air temperature and Dad's displeasure! We did survive. Maybe we broke Dad; he ran for Union County Sheriff in 1961 and was elected and took office in 1963. His salary jumped from $1,800 to $6,000 a year.

Some of the things we got to do at a very young age were steering the 8N Ford tractor in the hay field while pulling the hay wagon. That was at an age of seven or eight. Dad made sure we were on a level surface, and the tractor was in first gear. We sure thought we were in tall cotton. I was selected many times to pull the hay fork back after the hay was dumped into the loft. As we got older, around 13 or 14 years of age, we began loading hay on the wagon or stacking hay in the barn loft. It sure was an effective bodybuilding exercise.

We would help Mom with her canning, gathering eggs, feeding the livestock, and picking blackberries and strawberries. We would help cultivate and harvest produce out of the large garden. That was the way most of the kids in rural America grew up. We were all poor, but we didn't realize it. We were richly blessed with a stable home life. We developed a good work ethic as a result of having responsibilities. Bruce and I had clothing, albeit on a limited basis. We each had two pairs of bib overalls and a pair of shoes apiece. Mom would patch or repair them when necessary. We may have been poor, but we knew we were loved, and we knew we would be taken care of. Dad's annual salary in the '30s was $1,800 per year. $150 a month wouldn't go very far now. I can remember Mom going to the Daniels store in Jonesboro and coming out with three large sacks of groceries for just $5. A dollar was a dollar then!

One day, Dad was busy, and we were bored. We had a grain drill with the name JOHN DEERE VAN BRUNT painted on it. The manufacturer was John Deere. We had the brilliant idea of scratching out some of the letters on the drill. We scratched out the J, two Ns, the V, and the B to make it read "OH DEERE A RUNT." Mom and Dad

didn't find it as amusing as we did, but years later they admitted it was funny. That drill was used for many more years with its new name, "OH DEERE A RUNT" inscribed on it.

In the 1950s, using a one-row corn picker meant several rows of corn would be knocked down while opening a field. Bruce and I were always designated to pick the "down" rows. As we picked up the stalks and pulled the ears of corn off, we would then throw the ears of corn into the narrow 50-bushel wagon. Sometimes, Dad would get too far ahead of the tractor or the horses. Once, we got a little lazy and let the wagon get so far ahead that we hit Dad right on the head. That turned out to be one day we would remember for life. To make matters worse, a few days later, Dad was standing in the front of the wagon, and he asked me to pull the wagon forward. For some reason, (to this day I haven't figured out why) I decided to stop the tractor. Dad was standing in the front of the wagon. He fell over the front of the wagon right onto the tongue. I still can hear the groan he let out as he hit! Thank the good Lord he was only slightly bruised. Bruce and I have blocked out what our punishment was for those two dumb incidents.

The most wonderful thing about working alongside Dad and Mom are the memories of the funny incidents, as well as those that weren't so funny. Bruce and I have had so many occasions to talk about those times with Dad and Mom. I've had some people say to me, "How nice you have that to share." Many children grow up, especially those who lived in cities, who basically just watched their parents go to work. They don't have those memories to share later in life. We were certainly blessed!

THE MEISENHEIMERS

Two really special people in our lives were the Meisenheimers—Doug and Anna (Annie). They were like grandparents to us. We literally grew up under their feet. We lived about a mile away just off the Cape Road. Doug, Annie, and Mom and Dad would work together in their farming operations, and Bruce and I helped out quite a bit.

Every time I would arrive at their house, I would hear Annie say, "Hi, Ronnie." They had lost their son Fred during WWII when he was in his early 20s. "Hard work" was their motto. Their 160-acre farm was very hilly. However, they knew how to manage erosion by utilizing grass waterways. Many times, they would place tree branches crossways and place straw or hay to collect or slow the water run-off. Annie also had some flat land which accounted for another 30 acres just east of their farm on Airport Lane near Dutch Creek. In addition, they owned some land on the old Goodman place just above their farm on Plank Hill.

Annie & Doug Meisenheimer

The Meisenheimers were very special to our family. Bruce and I adored them. Doug and Anne were the hardest working people that I have ever known. They would get up at 3:00 - 4:00 a.m. every day. I used to think that was early. (I've found myself doing the same thing in my late 70s.) They milked six cows twice daily by hand. During summer months, Annie had a large garden like ours and would start working early in her garden while it was still cool. After milking, she would use a separator to separate the milk fat (cream) from the whole milk. I can remember drinking buttermilk at Annie's, but I never cultivated a taste for it. My dad enjoyed buttermilk. Most people today drink skim, 1% or 2% but not whole milk, and it's processed. But all the milk we drank on the farm was raw. As a kid we never thought much about it. We didn't know any different.

After collecting the cream, Annie would churn it into butter. The skim milk was used to mix in with oats to slop (feed) the hogs. She and Doug would save the whole milk for their own consumption. We did the same thing with our milk, but I don't remember Mom churning as much as Annie did. We bought most of our butter from the Daniel's store on the square in Jonesboro.

WORKING FOR DOUG MEISENHEIMER

Doug paid us $1 an hour to help him bale hay. We didn't have as much hay as Doug, but our grain crops were about the same acreage. Doug had milk cows, and we raised sheep, hogs, and cattle. The sheep farming was a pain in the butt. They were so vulnerable to wild dog attacks and other large varmints. They would get caught by blackberry briars, and many times, would not even try to break themselves loose. If they laid downhill on their sides, oftentimes, they could not get back up. In other words, they required a lot of care.

When I worked at hay making, I made $12 in one day. That sounds funny now, but $12 went a long way in the '50s. My grade school coach would give the ball players 15 cents after a game, and that would buy us a coke and a bag of peanuts at the Twins Cafe on the square in Jonesboro. One time, my second grandpa, Doug Meisenheimer gave me $5 to buy an ice cream cone at the Twins Cafe. I went in, and he waited on me to come out with his change. When I came out, Doug said, "Do you have my change?" I said, "No, Mr. Hoss. Just keep the change." I guess I was playing big shot or didn't know the value of $5. The change coming was $4.95. Doug went in, and I'm sure Mr. Earl Hoss had the change ready. Just imagine 5 cents for an ice cream cone, or 15 cents for a coke and a bag of peanuts. That's why $12 was a nice pay check.

Our duties were about the same working with Dad on the farm as they were working for Doug. We made hay, scooped grain, and combined and baled hay with the same equipment that we used at Doug's. We co-owned the New Holland bailer with Doug.

Doug raised a lot of wheat, corn, and oats and usually had about 40 to 50 acres of clover that we would help him bale. Doug would round up four or five boys to help with the hay hauling. Bruce and I would usually help Doug round up some of our friends whom we knew would be good workers, and Doug loved kids. In the 1950s, the hay was baled in square bales, which would weigh between 60 and 70 pounds. One can see why we needed to be at least 13 or 14 years old to lift the bales. One July day, Bruce and I helped take in 1,000 bales. That was the day I made $12. We were exhausted. In July, the daytime temperature was always in the 90s and sometimes it even rose into the 100-degree range.

We boys started working at an early age, especially in the hay fields. Doug and Dad would let us steer their little 8N Ford tractors while pulling the hay or grain wagon. To ensure safety, we always did it only on level surfaces.

Labor in the '50s was often done by young boys. Doug's fields were very hilly. The tractor would be put in first gear "granny low", and older boys and adults would load the hay onto the wagon. If we were harvesting grain, we would pull the grain wagon to the grain bin.

HAY AND GRAIN SEASON

Hay and grain season was always an exciting time for Bruce and me. It was a way of life for us. Today's kids can't relate. If you asked them to do what we did, they might look at you and ask, "Are you crazy!?" It's hard for kids to relate to something they haven't lived through. In order for our parents to make a living, we all had to work. We never resented it. Sometimes, we'd miss out on some activity, but it was understood we were part of the operation. Grain and hay making is so much more automated today. $300,000 self-propelled combines can harvest hundreds of acres of grain in one day. Hay balers now roll up 1,000-1,500-pound round bales that are picked up by a prong mounted on the rear of the tractor. It used to take a week of good weather to harvest 60 acres. Our combines were all pull-type with a five or six-foot swath. Today's big combines have 18-20-foot swaths. Our small fields of 10-20 acres would be harvested in just a few minutes. Many farms today measure thousands of acres. Northern Illinois is a good example. While driving through Kansas to report to my first Navy duty station in Washington State, I was amazed at the size of the fields of wheat. One couldn't see to the end of the rows, they were so long.

The reason we liked working for the Meisenheimers was the food that Annie prepared: Open-faced sour cream pies, fried chicken, chicken and dumplings, fresh tomatoes, and other fruits and vegetables all grown on the farm. The drink was usually lemonade with fresh-squeezed lemons. Around 3 p.m. every day, Annie would have lemonade and a snack for us. She knew how to keep morale high. Life was so simple, compared to today.

On the 4th of July we would go to town, after we had worked all day, to attend the July 4th fireworks. We would be tired, but it was a physical tired. It seemed to be just what we needed to finish off the day. In those days, we didn't make it into town during the summer months very often. It's hard to relate to that today. We lived only 3 1/2 miles from Jonesboro. It just wasn't a priority. We had our neighbor families, and Bruce and my social life mainly consisted of the neighborhood boys. Neighborhood gatherings were the center of rural culture at that time.

Another of the jobs, besides pulling the hay and grain wagons, was shoveling grain with a scoop. Granted, we didn't do much scooping of grain until we reached age 11 or 12. We were too small and lacked the strength to scoop for 20 or 30 minutes. We still pulled the hay and grain wagons, but as 10-12-year-olds, we had the additional duty of scooping grain from the wagon into the old grain rooms. The metal grain bins were still not in use on the Meisenheimer or Fulenwider farms. The grain rooms were in the old barns. They would be boarded up with tongue and groove boards. Rodents were always a problem. Rodent poisons were used frequently, but the problem persisted, due to the large rodent population. I can remember Dad catching six- and seven-foot long blacksnakes and putting them into the grain rooms. Snakes are prolific feeders on the rodent population. Grandma Barber never assisted in this endeavor!

EARLY HAY MAKING

Following many years of making hay "in the loose," the hay baler debuted. I still have vivid memories of taking in loose hay. It was in the 1940s and very early 1950s. I was too little to help, so I enjoyed riding on the hay wagon. The hay was stacked to a height of 9 -10 feet. It was exciting to ride way up in the air. The wagons were specially designed in a concave pattern so the hay wouldn't slide off the wagon. I remember one load turned over on a slope that was too steep for the wagon. On steep slopes, the wagon would have to be driven straight down instead of sideways. I was glad I wasn't on those loads.

Our rakes were the old sulky rakes. The rakes would take the mowed hay and rake it into small windrows. The farmers had hay forks that had between three- and five-tine pitchforks. They would gather the windrows and stack them into large piles of hay. As the hay wagon approached each stack of hay, the farmers would load the loose hay onto the wagon. One farmer would stand on the wagon to distribute the hay evenly.

Hay would then be taken up into the barn by a two-prong fork by rope and pulley. This method of hay-making was time-consuming and required much labor. The advent of the hay baler brought a revolutionary method of making hay. I remember when Doug and Dad got a new hay baler. The hay baler was a New Holland. They are still around today, only much more modern. The baler meant the pitchfork and sulky rake would not be used as much. Hay would still be mowed and raked into windrows, but the hay baler had a conveyor with wire prongs that pulled the hay inside to be compressed into a rectangular bale and tied with either string or wire. The wire was superior, but one had better have gloves on. It made for easier loading onto the wagon. Men could work both sides of the wagon and load 60 to 70 bales within 30 minutes. The weight of the load would be about two tons. A load of loose hay would be about half the weight of baled hay because it was not compressed.

Doug would hire kids from town to help with the hay hauling. He loved having kids around him. Doug and Annie really enjoyed the entertainment the kids provided. Since they'd lost their only son, kids were very special to them. We usually got kids we knew from school to help. It would often be the basketball or football players at AJ. Some of the kids I invited were Don Ray, Ron Knupp, Jim Shephard, Tony Ferrell, Clyde Lingle, Jr., Bronel Jerrell, and Steve Tweedy. Those guys were good workers and very tough. We would all try to out-do each other throwing the hay bales. The hay was usually stacked four or five

bales high on the wagon. Some of the boys could go five high, but not me. I only weighed about 100 pounds and stood 5'1" tall at age 13. Tony Ferrell was about 5'6" at the same age. By my senior year, however, I had caught up with most of the boys, and I could hold my own with them. Poor old Ron Knupp was put up in the barn loft where it was hot and dusty. I can't remember, and neither can Ron, who gave him a chew of tobacco, but he got very sick. That certainly is one way to turn one away from chewing. I loved hay making with my high school friends. Memories like those don't fade.

On a good day, we could put 500-600 bales of hay into the barn. That method of making hay was replaced in the early to middle 1960s by elevators. The elevators were much faster and required less labor. In many ways, we missed the former way of taking up hay. Doug and Annie enjoyed the social gatherings and missed having the boys coming to the farm to work. We still needed labor, but we didn't need as many boys to work. With elevators we could unload hay or grain directly into the barn loft. Wagons were equipped to unload the grain directly into the elevator. I was glad to see the scoop use greatly diminished, and so was my back. I still have that scoop today as a reminder of the good old days!

THE MEISENHEIMER'S HIRED MAN ARLEY

We worked hard on the Meisenheimer farm, but we had some entertaining times observing Doug, Annie, and

Arley. None of them had hearing aids. Hearing problem are serious, but the handicap created some very funny incidents. Doug would give Arley a job to do that he wasn't excited about, and Arley would just cuss ol' Doug up one side and down the other. Doug's response was, "Huh?" whether he knew Arley was giving him the once over or not. When they would argue, it was so loud that it became comical. Arley, like Doug, was a very hard worker. He could scoop grain all day and never seem to tire. His right hand was missing all of the fingers, so it was an amazing thing to watch. He learned to use his handicapped hand very effectively. He could tie a knot on hay rope (one-inch in diameter) with ease.

One day, we were in the barn restacking some hay, and I found a hen's nest. I said to Doug and Arley, "I dare you to eat those two raw eggs." The temperature during the summer in the old barn loft was at least 95 degrees. Doug and Arley wasted no time. They picked up the two eggs, cracked them open, and ate them. The eggs were very warm, but they didn't even check to see if they were fresh.

This is a story I love to tell. I call it "Annie vs. Arley." Arley, the Meisenheimers hired man, would sometimes get lax in his personal hygiene, especially bathing. The shower in the basement was where he was supposed to bathe, but often, Arley would skip showering and go directly to bed. Can you imagine how dirty a person would be after working and sweating all day in hay or grain? He thought he had Annie fooled, but he didn't. When it came time for the bed sheets to be washed, Annie would find out. His sheets would always be very dirty. She would tie into him, as you can imagine, and Arley would get mad, move out, and sleep in his car. His car had to be very uncomfortable, especially during the summer months. Annie would say, "We have paid that man $6,000 over the last ten years, and this is the appreciation we get!" On Arley's behalf, he worked 75 hours per week for $600 a year, which came to around $12 a week. Arley did get room and board, at least until he moved out. Imagine getting paid $50 a month. Even in the 1950s, that was not much of a salary. Eventually, Arley would agree to the rules and get his room back. During the weeks in his car, Arley would be allowed to use the shower or the farm pond, whichever he chose. He also would eat with Doug and Annie but rarely said a word at lunch or dinner. The situation was comical but also a little sad. Arley would talk to me, but only one-on-one, with no other people around.

BERRY-PICKING

Doug farmed 14-16 hours a day. He loved farming with his little 8N Ford tractor. He loved plowing, disking, planting, and baling hay. The one thing he didn't like was helping Annie in her garden. One day, during strawberry season, she asked Doug to help pick some strawberries. Annie worked hard in her large beautiful garden and took great pride in it. But Doug wasn't pleased with the assignment of picking berries. He started picking berries, and not just the ripe ones. He picked the green ones, too. If I remember correctly, he brought in about six quarts of the most beautiful red and green berries that you have ever seen. Annie took one look at the containers and said, "All you want to do is keep your damned a... on the seat of a tractor all day." She ran him out of the yard. I guess that worked for Doug. I don't think he ever picked another berry for Annie.

DOUG'S COMBINING EXPERIENCE

Doug was a 5'7" 212-pound man. He had a problem moving his head to either side. One 4th of July, he tried to combine, and it was 104 degrees. The Fulenwiders were not available because we were celebrating with family. We usually did all of Doug's combining because of his disability. He could do a pretty good job when it came to baling hay, but he must have decided that he could combine, too. Immediately after he started, he had problems maneuvering the levers. He had gotten too much straw on the conveyor and had stopped up the cylinder bars. The straw had to be removed manually, a very hot and dirty job. Doug got over-heated, climbed off the combine, and made his way to the house. He told Annie, "I am so sick." He was probably nearing heat exhaustion. Annie immediately took him to the basement, had him remove his clothes, put him under the shower, and ran cold water on him for several minutes. The tough German recovered, but he never combined again without Jean and his two boys. Annie may have remembered the strawberry incident and was tempted to drown him. What a couple! I'm so thankful I got to enjoy them for so many years.

EVENING TELEVISION

Television time was usually later in the evening. Doug, Annie, and Arley would settle in after a late supper to watch T.V. I can remember arriving at the Meisenheimer home early in the day, usually around 6 a.m. I would go to the door to see if everybody was ready to start the day's work. No one would ever be up before Doug and Annie. Usually, their day started around 3 or 4 a.m. One day was different. Reaching the door, I heard the television blasting, and in the chairs were the three of them sound asleep still in their clothes. They had never made it to bed. It still makes me smile.

THE NEW HOME (1952)

Doug and Annie built a new home in 1952. Upon completion of the new one, the old house was torn down. The new home came with nice new appliances and plumbing which meant they would have running water, a shower in the basement, and another bathroom with sink, stool, and tub. The kitchen had a sink with running water. As an 11-year-old, I was fascinated watching a new home being built. I was at Doug and Annie's house two or three days a week. School was out for the summer, so it worked well with my schedule and Doug's also. I know it sounds crazy. Kids today are not so isolated. They wouldn't think anything about a house being built. They are busy with soccer, baseball, sports camps, and a myriad of other things that were not available to the rural kids of my childhood days. They go camping, travel to other countries, visit educational facilities, and so many other places. We had 4H clubs and Boy Scouts, but nothing like the many activities today. But I was thrilled to see a house go up. I would bring my lunch bucket and stay all day.

Doug & Annie Meisenheimer in their new home.

Chapter 4

Random Memories

INTERESTING THINGS THE OLD GERMANS SAID

Many of the German immigrants who entered the United States in the 1880s and 1890s and settled in our area never learned to speak English. In the 1940s, I remember two or three who only spoke German. My mom's best friend, Jo Morgan's father didn't speak English. The ones who did speak English were interesting to listen to. Many of the farmers and country people would say things according to the sound of the words. They never learned to read or spell. Their vocabularies were very limited. Most didn't have good educations. Many children would attend school only a few months out of the year. Many stayed on the farm and worked to help provide for the family's needs.

Here are a few interesting examples:

Our neighbor Bill: "Runty, did you read that arr-tick-le in yesterday's paper?" His wife, Nora: "That will learn them a think or two."

Harold, a local farmer: "That sow had ten pigs and et every one of them."

Many of the old timers would say kitchen "zink" instead of kitchen sink. That is the way they heard the word.

Doug would say: "There hain't a thing wrong with that there car." He called his machinery – "sheenery."

Many people would use the word "plum." My dad used it often.

"He went plum over the hill the last time I saw him." "It's just plum run down. The car won't run anymore."

Here's a statement I still hear today. "We are fixin' to go to town."

Another commonly misused word was "know." Many people would say, "I knowed that." "He knowed that he should not have did that."

I also heard a lot of people say "chester drawers" for chest of drawers. I'm pretty sure that I said it myself.

"You-uns" and "yous" were often substituted for "you." Are "you-uns" going to town?" "What do yous want to eat tonight?" Words were commonly misused in rural areas in the 1940s and 1950s. There are people in some areas who still talk that way.

One of Bruce's friends talked about getting into a fight with another boy on the Jonesboro square. Here's how Bruce said the conversation went: "He wrech out to hit me, and I got all het up, and we fit all over the park." "Wrech" was used a lot for reach.

Dad told this one about a German immigrant in Jonesboro when he discussed feeding his horse named Dewey. "I ran down the ladder and up into the loft, and I threw old Dewey out the loft some hay." Poor Dewey. That same immigrant got mad about something that Cecil Norris, the undertaker at Norris & Son Funeral Home, had done to him. He went into the funeral home on the square in Jonesboro, pointed his finger at Cecil and said, "You will never bury me, as long as I live!" He walked out so mad, but he got his point across, because Cecil never buried him as long as he lived!

SOME FUNNY MEMORIES

I will never forget an incident with Mom and our hired man's wife, Martha Trammel. Dad had just purchased several ten-pound tomato containers. The containers were placed just outside the front entrance to our house. Early one morning, prior to packing tomatoes, Mom and Mrs. Trammel discovered a black snake that had gotten into the containers. Mom immediately entered the house, grabbed the rifle, came out, and started shooting at the containers. After a few minutes, she finally hit the snake and killed it. What was not so good was the fact that she had shot up several of the containers. That was a costly snake. Dad was not so happy because all they would have had to do was separate the containers. Maybe Mom's fear of snakes overrode her thinking process. It wasn't as funny at the time as it was, many years later, when Dad told the story.

In the '50s, my grandmother Barber came to stay with us quite regularly, and she would often help with the chores. One day, she went to the barn to gather eggs, as she had done many other times. That day was different, however, because as she reached into a nest to pick up an egg, she felt something cold. It was a large black snake that had just placed one of the eggs into its mouth. I was home, and I turned and saw Grandma running away, waving her apron, and screaming, "Oh, my gosh! Oh, my gosh! Grandma never gathered another egg. A few years later, we were all outside, sitting underneath our 150-year-old elm tree. In the summer months, before air conditioning, we would go outside until it would cool down. That particular evening, over sixty years ago, something happened that I will never forget. We were all having a good time visiting: Mom, Dad, Grandma, Bruce, and me—when a seven-foot black snake fell out of the elm tree right in front of Grandma. She was scared out of her wits and scampered into the house. That was the last time she sat outside, which limited the places she could go on the farm. One day, she decided it was time to go back home to Murphysboro. I honestly didn't blame her.

I used to go to Grandma and Grandpa Barbers' in the summer months, when school was out. Grandpa never drove a car, so he walked all over Murphysboro. I had the privilege, at a young age, to go to Riverside Park and watch semi-pro baseball. It was somewhat like going to Rent One Park now. There were a number of those teams around the country at that time. I know West Frankfort had a team. It was always so much fun being with Grandpa. After the games, we would walk back to Elm Street where they lived in an apartment. Grandpa was a very good clothing salesman for Recthter Brothers Department Store on Walnut Street. He had the gift of gab which helped him sell a lot of clothing. Also, Grandpa was so superstitious that if we saw a black cat in front of us, we would have to turn around and go around the block the other way.

With Grandma, I had totally different experiences. She didn't drive either, but we would go downtown, shop, then take in a movie, which we used to call a "picture show." I saw my first 3-D movie, and it was so good. I was ducking under my seat all through the show because everything was flying out at us. 3-D movies are rare today. You'd think that modern technology would make them very popular. I remember each of us being issued a special pair of glasses. I still have fond memories of those kind of movies.

This next event also took place in downtown Murphysboro on Walnut Street. In the early 1950s, we didn't have a TV, so, on Saturday night, Grandma and I would go to downtown Murphysboro and watch TV at one of the appliance stores. The appliance store would set up the TV, and we would watch from outside the show window. They would wire the sound so we could all hear the program. It sounds like we were in Backwoods U.S.A. I told you, we were poor and didn't realize it. It was great entertainment. Fifteen or twenty people would be sitting outside on the street on the foldup chairs we'd brought with us. Televisions were very expensive when they first came out, so there was no way we could have purchased one.

The shows we watched were "Dragnet" and "Saturday Night Wrestling." We only had two channels – St. Louis and Memphis. Everything was in black and white. Sometimes, the shows would be very "snowy" if the aerial antenna was not set right. We didn't have remote control;

we had a rotor that turned the aerial, and they weren't always reliable. Sometimes, people would get upset if the appliance store wasn't paying attention and the program got snowy. We couldn't say much, because it was free. The appliance store people would usually fix the problem after someone tapped on the door. The store owner definitely wanted everything to go well, because he was trying to sell TVs. A black and white TV cost around $500 or $600 in the '50s. Color TVs were available, but they were too expensive for most rural Americans. My wealthy Uncle Roscoe had a color TV in the late '50s. He was a St. Louis dentist, and he could afford one. The cost was between $6,000 and $8,000. The color was poor, and the picture was grainy, but I was amazed that we could see programs in color.

THE CAR THIEF

We were awakened one fall night by the loud sound of a car horn. We immediately thought someone was in our car trying to hot wire and steal it. We had an old 12-gauge LC Smith shotgun that Dad grabbed as he went out in the yard. When he approached the car, up popped our German Shepherd. One of the windows had been left down, and King decided to make himself at home. He probably bumped the horn as he entered the car. It was probably as frightening to King as it was to us!

WOODEN WALL PHONES

Most families in the '50s had wooden wall-mounted phones. Those were the days of party lines. We had a party line of six families. You could always count on two of the ladies to pick up the phone and listen, no matter whom a call was intended for. When it rang, immediately, Anna or Nora would pick up the phone. We usually could tell who was on the line. Maybe they were nosy or just bored, or maybe they just wanted to pick up important information about local activities. A phone call to their neighbors could provide more up-to-date information than the newspaper or radio. Many times, we would say, "Anna (or Nora), this is a private call," and we would hear a click as the phone was put down.

Most of our calls were local—Union County. Long distance calls were prohibitively expensive. If you did want to make a long-distance call, you would give the operator the number. It would take a little while until you finally got the party you were calling. Next you would receive a huge bill from Bell telephone, which I believe was the only phone company in the country.

If one wanted to communicate outside of their area, it was usually done by letter. Compared to our ability to e-mail and text today, it was amazingly low-tech. We communicated with Grandma Barber that way, most of the time. It's easy to see why the United States Postal Service did so well in those years. After Christmas, we would write thank you cards to all of my aunts. Since Dad had nine sisters, that was the best way for us to communicate.

Local calls were simple. For example, if the call was intended for someone whose "number" was two shorts and one long, the person would do two shorts and one long crank on the wooden phone. If anyone wanted to make a long-distance call, they would have to go through an operator. For a long-distance call, an operator would ask, "What city?" Or if someone had the prefix Chi (as in CHI-3324), they could call directly into the city of Chicago. That is the way I remember it working.

In the '60s, the rotary phones and touch-tone phones no longer needed to go through an operator. However, it still remained expensive.

Radio in Rural Southern Illinois

In the '50s, we finally got electricity. No longer did Bruce and I have to study by kerosene lamps or use the facility called the outhouse. There is nothing worse than waking up on a cold winter's night to make the trip to the outdoor facility. In the 1930s, the Rural Electrification Authority (REA) was established, but we didn't get electricity until 1951. That was the main driving force in the beginning of radio. It gave us so much access to modernizing farm operations and opened up a myriad of new conveniences.

I remember getting our first radio. It was a huge box. It gave us access to so many new shows like "Burns and Allen," "Red Skelton," and "Bob Hope." One of the main things Dad, Bruce, and I listened to were the fights on Wednesday and Friday nights. Listening to Joe Louis, Jersey Joe Walcott, and Rocky Marciano was really thrilling. One would have to have a great imagination. Kids today don't have to imagine now like we did. Television didn't exist yet. The '50s were the Golden Years of Radio. And we went from no electrical devices to access to local, national, and world news. Farmers like Dad could get market reports on all the commodities. Before, it would be days before they could get any information on prices for their crops and livestock.

In the '40s, we listened to the radio a lot. Those Joe Lewis fights were great. You could only hear the play-by-play, and Dad would be right there with us. A few years later, when we got our TV, we watched the Friday night fights. Rocky Marciano and Jersey Joe Walcott were great fighters. Dad even thought boxing might be a good way for his sons to vent their frustrations. It worked well until Bruce laid me out and bloodied my nose. I was out on a T.K.O. That was the end of the gloves; Mom burned them. Dad and the two boys lost the "Main Event."

A THANKSGIVING TO REMEMBER

In the early 1950s, we were still using a team of horses for some farming practices. We had a team of draft horses named Prince and Barney. They were Belgian horses. Mom and Dad said that when I was four or five years old, I would play around them in the barn, and they would just step over me or around me. They were very gentle. The horses were used primarily to plant corn and soybeans. They pulled a two-row planter. When harvesting corn, we had a one-row corn picker. In order to open a field, we had to run over some rows of corn. We called these the down rows. Those rows had to be picked by hand, which was my and Bruce's job. It was no fun at all. The old wagon that we had held about 50 bushels of ear corn. It was steel- wheeled and very narrow. The cold frosty days in the fall were sometimes brutal. We had gloves, but our hands would still get cold.

On Thanksgiving morning 1952, we were picking corn up from the down rows and using our horses because of the wet conditions in the 30- acre bottom land adjacent to the Old Cape Road just off of Route 127 south of Jonesboro. It was very cold and damp that day, and very cloudy. We started working about 9 a.m. At 10, it started snowing heavily. The weather forecast in those days was not very accurate. It was before most meteorologists had accurate instruments. Dad asked if I would like to walk the horses to the house. I said, "Yes, I would." It was a two-mile walk, and I didn't get cold at all. It was sure a neat experience for me as an 11-year-old. I felt so proud guiding those big beautiful horses up the Old Cape Road to the house. Prince and Barney probably weighed nearly a ton each. As small as I was, they looked huge. By 2 p.m., the snow was about 6" deep. Doug and Annie had already come over for Thanksgiving dinner. I still remember that morning vividly.

Chapter 5
Personal Observations and More Memories

THE CULTURE: YESTERDAY VS. TODAY

In those days, we didn't have all the distractions that are prevalent today. Televisions, cell phones, and video games have their benefits, but I believe they are robbing families of quality time. Many today have developed an obsession with cell phones and video games. Communication with family, friends, and school mates is suffering greatly, in my opinion. Almost everyone seems to have a cell phone in his hand. They are a wonderful invention if used for their main purpose. I'm old school, and it drives me nuts to see kids sitting in groups of five or six, and every one of them is on his cell phone. It would be so nice if they were communicating among themselves with face-to-face conversation. A survey showed that kids spend an average of 4 1/2 hours a day with their cell phones either texting, talking, or playing video games.

Simplicity was the norm in the '40s and '50s. I'm not advocating going back to the past, although I would like to see improvement in our communication in homes, schools, and businesses. I know that many families today have good family time and family relationships. I know of young people who have chores to do. My prayer is that families will understand the value of quality family time. Life is so much more complex today, and it is important to stay focused on quality time together. Growing up in America today has many more cultural challenges than in the past.

My good friend Dr. John Earnhart and I talked about how our grandparents said the same thing. They would say, "I just don't know what the young people are going do with all the evil things going on today." They had a point. However, we are in a tremendous cultural change in America. Dr. Earnhart, whom I admire greatly, said, "The youth will make a transition as we have." I pray that this will be the case. Never have we had this much change in such a short time. Many parents that are doing a great job of rearing their kids, but they have the added responsibility of knowing what is going on with their children. It is definitely much more difficult for them than for our parents back in the 1950s.

My mother Maxine was a great person, a good Christian woman, and a loving mother. She would do anything for Bruce and me and had the love and respect of both of us. She died February 10th, 2005, one day shy of her 89th birthday. She is greatly missed.

She was the parent, and Bruce and I were the children. Like John Rosemond stated, "'No' meant 'no.'" She wasn't interested in being our friend or our buddy. She believed and practiced the old-school approach to discipline. When she said, "Ronald Jean come here!" I knew that I had overstepped my boundaries. Mom wasn't too big on the belt; she preferred the hickory switch that would wrap around the calves of one's legs. It would sting and was effective. Our respect for Mom and Dad stood the test of time. As we grew older, we always looked up to both of them.

THE LAKE HILL/MEISENHEIMER NEIGHBORHOOD BOYS

We were fortunate to have had great neighbors. The farms in the Lake Hill region were all 40-80-acre farms— all very small by today's standards. Farms today measure 2,000-3,000 acres. One farm in the Ware/McClure area is 12,000 to 14,000 acres. Our farm was joined on three sides by neighbors—all with small acreage. There were about ten neighborhood boys whom Bruce and I would play with on Saturdays and Sunday afternoons.

Some of the games we played might be considered dangerous—corn cob fights around the barn and barn lot. We would divide up in teams.

There were never any winners or losers, unless one of us got hit in the eye and had to drop out. We each got an allotment of corn cobs, and we would play for an hour or two. The goal was to give as many stinging hits as we could. It hurt quite a bit to get hit on the head, chin, eyes, or neck. The only real danger was getting hit in the eye. We never thought to wear goggles for protection. What really got rough was when we used cobs that had dried mud or dried cow dung on them. I don't remember anyone ever getting seriously hurt. The good Lord was watching over us!

Another game we played was football in the clover or alfalfa hay fields. We didn't play touch football; we played tackle football. It hurt like the dickens to get tackled, but we were young and felt invincible. Once again, I don't remember anyone getting hurt very badly. We always played football in the fall of the year. The corn cob fights happened in late fall and winter months.

The other game we played in the winter was basketball in Edwin (Sonny) Eddleman's barn. My good childhood friends Larry Morgan and Sonny Eddleman and I would play for hours in his barn because it had a nice solid floor. Sonny's goal was regulation height, and we had an area almost half the size of a small grade-school gym. On the bitter cold days, we would stack hay around the perimeter of the barn to block off the bitter cold air.

The main basketball game we played was "Horse." It helped pass the time on long winter days and added good physical exercise to our regular farm chores and activities.

Other activities Bruce and I did around our home included making stilts and walking around the yard and barnyard. It was a lot of fun. We also made bows and arrows and played "cowboys and Indians." Hickory made the best bows because they would bend quite easily without breaking. We usually used kite string for the bows. Then we'd find some straight branches to make our arrows. We did try to wear goggles for safety, but I doubt that we were ever in any danger, because we weren't very accurate. One more activity I remember was crushing cans around our shoes and walking around with them. We must have been terribly bored because I can't understand why we ever found that fun. Maybe the sound of the clatter on the ground was intriguing.

A Few More Memories that Stand Out

Once, I talked Dad into buying me a mushroom kit for $50. I was going to grow mushrooms and make a fortune. I grew one mushroom. I had a nice place to work, but I didn't allow for mice eating the mushroom spawn. I was ten years old with great expectations. My dad and mom were so good to allow me to try things. That $50 would be like $500 today. I know my parents sacrificed for me.

I have a vivid memory of being scared to death after watching the movie *Wolfman Meets Frankenstein* at the Doll Theatre in Jonesboro. What made it so scary was that I had to walk from the Jonesboro Square all the way down to Williford Road to the Dodd residence where Mom and Dad were. It was close to a mile. I was a small child, and I kept seeing creatures in my mind. If a dog had jumped out in front of me, I would still be running. Those old black and white motion pictures with Boris Karloff were really scary.

Mom used to say this to us boys, "I don't want either of you to go swimming until you learn how." Bruce and I had a smart response. "Mom, how can you learn to swim without swimming?" She meant in a properly controlled environment with a life guard or some other supervision. We both knew that, but a smart response was more fun. She said the same thing about driving. "Don't drive until you learn how." Another of Mom's famous statements was "You boys, make sure you have clean underwear on, in case you are in an accident." We had a smart response for that, too. You can imagine what it was.

I remember vividly going to Mom and Dad's good friends' business in Jonesboro. The business was the Dixie Barbeque. The establishment opened in 1947 and is still one of the finest restaurants in Southern Illinois. In 1949, I was told to go to the Dixie after school, and George and Bea Ferguson would watch me until Mom and Dad arrived later. But I decided I would go to my good friend's house over on North Main. Steve Tweedy lived about a mile from the Dixie. Mom and Dad showed up at the Dixie, and there was no Ronald. To this day, I can't remember how they found me. I do remember the belt, however. Not so brilliant on my part.

Christmas in the early 1950s was one of my favorite times. One year, I got a Roy Rogers double holster gun set. It had a genuine leather holster with pearl handle guns. I was Roy Rogers for a long time. On another great Christmas, I got a Lionel train, and another I got a Red Ryder (Daisy) BB gun, but my all-time favorite was the Roy Rogers set.

I played basketball in 1952-53 and 53-54 for the Jonesboro Bulldogs. Those are some of my favorite memories ever. We had so much fun playing ball in those tiny gyms with six-foot lanes and the double-time lines. The Lick Creek gym today seems very small, but it would be considered big compared to those old gymnasiums. Cobden, Alto Pass, and Dongola were all very tiny. The old gym at Anna Jr. High was one of the larger gyms during the '40s and '50s.

I always loved my mom's cooking. I remember her in her apron cooking and singing Christian songs. She loved to cook for her family, and did so, well into my 60s. My wife, Paula, is a good cook, just like Mom. I was so blessed then, and I still am today.

Mom and I would cultivate with a garden hoe around the plants. Once in a while, we would accidentally chop down a tomato or pepper plant. We would look at each other and mischievously place the plant back in the ground so Dad wouldn't detect a plant missing. If he saw a plant wilting, he would think it was a cut worm. Who would suspect mother and son in crime together?

I remember the cold winter nights on the old Lake Hill farm. We didn't have insulation in the late '40s, so the cold winter air made its way into our rooms. We had a floor furnace; however, the warm air didn't make it into the bedrooms at night. Mom would wrap warm irons in small blankets to get our feet warm, at least until we went to sleep. We slept under a couple layers of blankets and survived. Tough times don't last, but tough people do. We were tough, because we had to be.

I have great memories of my best friends, Tony Ferrell, Steve Tweedy, and Larry Morgan. The best memory I have is about Tony. Once, when he stayed all night at our farm, we went walking around all over the farm. It was the night before our eighth-grade graduation. It was late May, and we came upon a black animal with a long white streak down its back. Before we could holler, "Skunk!" we were sprayed with an unforgettably intense odor. In those days, none of us had more than one pair of shoes. Skunk odor, as everyone knows, is impossible to get out of anything. When we got dressed for graduation, we put on clean clothes, but our shoes still reeked of skunk. We put perfume all over them and everyone survived the unpleasant graduation ceremony. It was a tradition at graduation to will something back to the school. Tony and I were happy to bequeath that skunk smell to the next class.

I loved playing "pitch" with my grandpa Fulenwider. We would play for hours, and I loved every minute of it. He also carved things for me out of small tree limbs. One particular gift he gave me was a flute carved out of a Pawpaw branch. He had a way of sliding the wood out of the bark shell. He would put holes in the cylinder and plug the front of it sort of like a clarinet. It was impressive.

Another memory that is still very vivid is the time we went over to the old Dirkheimer farm (that my brother later bought). Dad told us we were going to rob a beehive located in the lower portion of a certain tree. He told us that the bees would be dormant due to the cold temperature. Without a smoker or anything, we started removing the honey with gloved hands. The temperature was in the high '20s—definitely cold. No sooner had we started than the bees began swarming all around us. Bruce and I ran like scared rabbits. Dad was in his late 40s at that time and couldn't run as fast as us. He got stung at least four or five times. The one that stung him on the edge of his eye really got his attention. The wild honey robbery came to a fast end. We didn't bring any honey home—only bee stings. Bruce and I got stung on our hands and arms, but the sting near Dad's eye caused it to swell completely shut. We kept wanting to ask Dad about bees being dormant, but we couldn't bring ourselves to do it when he looked at us with just one eye. How much we cherish those memories.

Another moment I shall not forget involved sharpening fence posts. We had a large 16-pound mallet that was used to drive fence posts into the ground. But one day, things didn't go well. Dad asked Bruce to hammer some fence posts into the ground. Dad said, "I will hold the fence post while you boys drive it into the ground." That ended up being a bad idea. Bruce did a pretty good job for a while until he got tired. He raised the mallet, missed the fence post, and caught Dad right across the shoulder. Thank goodness, he was ok. He hollered, "You birds get out of the way! I will do the hammering." I don't remember ever using the mallet with Dad again.

It makes me smile to remember Annie's milk money. Annie and Doug had separate bank accounts. They were very private about how much money they each had. Annie was in charge of the milk and egg production. Once, in the '50s, Annie was excited about the $1,800 she earned on the milk production. But Doug said, "You should have made $1,800 because you fed the milk cows my feed." It was a classic! Annie never said a word. They reminded me of Abbott and Costello or George and Gracie Allen. It was funny. When they passed away, both had accumulated a lot of money, and they left some to Dad. They never made a lot of money, however, they never spent much either. Sixty years of saving adds up.

I loved the little one-room schoolhouse on our land called the Lake Hill School—the one which had previously been called the Fulenwider School. I missed getting to go to it by one year, but I remember the slate chalkboards, the cloakroom, and ringing the old school bell that brought many of my aunts and my dad to school. (The old bell is still in use in my yard.) The basketball goal

I put up in one end of the school enabled me to play in the winter months when I was small and helped fuel my passion for basketball at an early age.

While in grade school, I collected baseball cards at the Bess Service Station right where the Hebrewzs Coffee House is located now. I collected cards like Stan Musial, Mickey Mantle, and other great players. They were called Topps cards, and I would get them when I purchased bubble gum. The gum was rolled out flat with the card underneath. We kids at the Jonesboro Grade School would take our cards to school and trade them for different players. I traded my Stan Musial for a number of other players; however, I kept the Mickey Mantle card. The cost of the bubble gum was 1 or 2 cents. I kept the cards for a few years, but once I got careless. Mom had told me to clean my room and pick up everything that was laying around. I didn't follow her instructions, and the cards were thrown away or burned with the trash. I also had Oscar Robertson's and Bob Pettit's autographs. Even those were gone. It sounds cruel on Mom's part, however, in the '50s, the cards weren't considered valuable. Fast forward to now. They are collector's items. We had no idea that the Mickey Mantle Triple Crown card would be worth thousands of dollars someday. I did have the privilege of talking to Oscar Robertson years later, while working with Bob Love. (As a boy, I would never have imagined I would get to meet "the Big O.")

"The lunchtime incident" occurred in 1952 when Doug and Annie were building their new home. Albert Sturgeon was the carpenter, and he carried a shiny black lunchbox. I hadn't seen a house being built before, so it was a fun thing for me to see. I usually brought my lunchbox and stayed the day. One day, I decided to paint my lunchbox black. I found a quart can of paint, and my finished work looked really nice. I arrived at Doug's early the next day with my bright new-looking lunchbox. Noon came, and I brought out my bright-looking lunchbox, just like Mr. Sturgeon's. When I opened it up, all of my food was covered with a black substance. I had painted my lunch box with tar! It went on just like paint, so I thought it was black paint. Albert and the carpenters got a big kick out of it! Thank goodness, Annie came to my aid with a nice lunch. A few months later, Albert was doing our indoor plumbing and he was still laughing about the tar bucket incident. Many years later, I was at Jumbo's restaurant in Vienna, and a man there asked me about a black lunchbox. I said, "How do you know about the black lunchbox?" The man was Doug Sturgeon, Albert's son. Since I'm from Jonesboro and that was in Vienna, it totally caught me off guard. The incident had taken place 65 years earlier. It was while I was coaching the Southern Illinois Lady Hoopsters (Johnson County Youth League). Maybe someone said my name, and he remembered the story his dad had told him. Coincidentally, I have taught Albert's great-grandchildren Dylan and Kennedy in my physical education classes at Lick Creek. Doug's daughter-in-law Amy Sturgeon was our teacher's aide, so she and I have also had a laugh about the old lunchbox.

Once, we had a pancake breakfast on the square right in front of the Twins Cafe. (Today there is a flower shop in the location.) We were all so excited, especially the grade school kids, because Aunt Jemima herself would be in Jonesboro, cooking her famous pancakes. It wasn't until years later I found out there were dozens of other

Aunt Jemimas all over the United States. We were a little naïve, but we sure enjoyed the bustling in Jonesboro that day. Life was pretty simple but still provided lots of happy memories.

Chapter 6
Good Childhood Leads to Strong Caring Adults

VALUE OF SMALL COMMUNITIES

The number of small rural communities has diminished somewhat, but many are still around today. One advantage of a small community is that people knew one another. Everyone watched out for each other. Lick Creek, where I teach, reminds me so much of my own childhood on the farm. If anyone got sick, someone was always available to help. My mom had a neighbor named Nora Hoover who was like a mother to all of us, especially to my mom. Nora was much older than Mom but was always available to assist during her pregnancies and when Bruce and I got sick. She was the one who looked after us when Mom had to help Dad with the peach harvest.

Another wonderful thing about living in rural America was the safety and security we had. I've mentioned previously about thumbing home after basketball practice. Today, we wouldn't consider letting our kids do something like that. Also, when we weren't in school, at the dinner table, or at church, we were outside playing. The neighborhood boys gathered to play football and many other games. We invented amazing contraptions, built forts and all kinds of other stuff, climbed around in the old silica mines, discovered interesting bugs and birds, and traipsed off on day-long trips. I could ride my bike all the way to Mill Creek and back. The trip from the farm off the old Cape Road to Mill Creek was 10 or 12 miles. Mom

Bottom sitting: Mike & Ronald. Sitting on bike: Jan in front and Bruce in the back.

would just say, "Be back before dark." Imagine riding a bike down Route 127 to Mill Creek in 2019. We knew how to take care of ourselves, with the Lord's help. We always knew where to find an adult quickly if one of us got into trouble. I can remember walking up and down creeks searching for tadpoles, frogs, and other types of animals. Once in a while, we would encounter snake; most were not poisonous (except for the water moccasins). We enjoyed fishing in Dutch Creek. It was so much fun catching the little sun perch. We never caught anything larger than four inches in length or weighing more than six or eight ounces. If we would have cleaned them, there wouldn't have been enough to feast on. When we got thirsty, we would drink out of the creek. We never carried a thermos bottle, and there was no such thing as bottled water. I never got sick from drinking creek water. In fact, it was very refreshing. With our water supply so close, we were able to play outside longer. Today, the proliferation of pesticide and fertilizer run-off would make it dangerous. But looking back after almost 60 years, I am grateful to have had such a wonderful childhood.

THE GOLDEN RULE

For us, the Golden Rule meant that we should be kind to our neighbors, all of whom looked pretty much like us, went to the same churches every Sunday, ate the same mashed potatoes, home-grown chicken, and butchered beef and pork. I can't help wondering what the world would be like if all the world's kids were well-fed, safe, and loved. We ate mostly organic foods. Today, American kids are fed a steady diet of processed "junk" food. In my opinion, this is why we have so much sickness and obesity. We have the ability to do more for children, but greed, lack of compassion, and our political system have misplaced our priorities.

Feeding and clothing the family and caring for our home was a full-time job for my mother. Back in the '40s and '50s, most rural mothers worked at home and on the farm. Each one had to be a wife, mother, nutritionist, tutor, designer, seamstress, decorator, and all around handy-woman. Mom was always available to help Bruce and me with our homework. She was also active with the school's Parent Teacher Association (PTA). Mom made sure we were always well-fed and had our clothes washed and pressed. Most of the time, we wore bib overalls to school. If they wore out, Mom would patch the knees to make them last as long as possible. She helped us with our school projects, got us over the hump learning the states, capitals, and times tables. Mom also spent untold hours working with the school, the church, and auxiliaries.

Holidays were expendable, as work took priority over celebrations. We never celebrated my birthday on June 14th. We were always in the barley, wheat, or oats fields combining or in the hay field making hay. I kidded Mom about it when she was in her '80s and she said, "Son, I'm so sorry." I didn't mean to make her feel bad. I reminded her that she usually managed to bake a cake and have a little party. Sometimes we even had homemade ice cream. The party was not always on June 14th because of farm work. Sometimes it would be on Sunday or a day that the rain prevented us from working. Truthfully though, we rarely celebrated July 4th because of grain harvest or hay making. The fireworks would be held at the Anna City Park around 9 p.m., but after working all day in the heat, we were too tired to attend anyway.

WEALTH

Back in rural Illinois in the '40s and '50s, wealth, in terms of money and property was almost non-existent. However, people survived without much money because they were able to produce much of their food in gardens. Mom would can many quarts of fruits and vegetables. We picked wild blackberries and dew berries which were also canned. We had apple and pear trees, so Mom would can apples and pears. We had a large copper kettle for making apple butter. We had chickens for our meat and eggs. We had a couple of milk cows to supply our dairy products. Mom would churn butter, and we had milk for cooking and drinking. We didn't buy many products like

Maxine Fulenwider, my mom.

candy, cakes, or soda. The only things we really had to purchase were staples like sugar, salt, and condiments. We had plenty of nutrient-rich food. Most of it was organic without additives or preservatives.

HEALTH

The main health issues in the 1950s were polio and tuberculosis (TB). I was lucky to avoid both diseases. My brother Bruce had TB in his early 20s, while in the US Navy. TB required a quarantine, and he spent quite a while in the San Diego Naval Hospital. Polio struck a number of children in the Union County area. When the Salk vaccine was introduced, the occurrence of polio was greatly reduced. Colds and fevers were common in children during the '50s, but it doesn't seem like they were as common as they are today. Poor nutrition contributes to childhood disease. Also, today, there are hundreds of drugs to treat illnesses. Anyone my age can remember only a few medicines. One was castor oil, which Dad loved to administer to Bruce and me. Mom would mix it with orange juice, but orange juice is a weak disguise for the distasteful flavor of castor oil. It was usually thrown right back up. To this day, I can't stand the smell of castor oil. Dad had the notion it was a cure-all for everything, but I don't recall him ever taking it himself. Mom and Dad used kerosene for treating cuts and wounds. I stepped on a nail once, and Mom put my foot into a pail of kerosene. It worked. In addition, cod liver oil, Epsom salts, Vaseline petroleum jelly, milk of magnesia, and Vicks VapoRub were about all we used. That's a far cry from the countless drugs available today.

Dad's Patience

The land we farmed was very hilly, especially on Doug's farm. Since we farmed with small 8N Ford tractors, we had problems getting up some of the steep slopes. The AC All-Crop combine was too heavy to get up the hills. Doug and Dad came up with a brilliant idea. They hooked the two 8N Ford tractors together with a chain, enabling them to get over the steep slopes. Bruce and I got the job of driving the front tractor. We were so excited, but we had to be very careful because of the tractor behind, driven by Dad. Our daydreaming would catch up with us once in a while. So many times, we would pop the chain and even break it—not a pleasant experience. I can still hear the frustration in Dad's voice, "You gourd heads are going to break me!" We got a lot more careful after a couple of unfortunate incidents. Dad was never known for great patience, but at least he didn't disown us. The Jonesboro, Vienna, New Simpson Hill, Cypress, Goreville, Buncombe, and Lick Creek kids know how patient I am. And now they know where the term "gourd head" comes from. I did hear it quite a few times.

SOCIAL TIME

When we weren't combining or in the hayfield, we would sometimes have an opportunity to go to the show (theater). The Doll Theater was the hot spot on the square in Jonesboro. We could get in for 15 cents and, for another dime, purchase enough candy and popcorn to hold us through a double-feature film.

Saturday night was bath time so everyone would be clean for Sunday church. Most stores were closed on Sunday—even grocery stores. In Cape Girardeau, Missouri, the "blue law" stayed in effect into the 1970s. Families went to their local churches for Sunday school first, followed by the pastor's sermon. Most families didn't go out to eat. Adults usually ended up inviting family or friends over for dinner and visited with one another while the kids played outside.

In the '50s, we read a lot of comic books like "Superman," "Captain Marvel," and "Wonder Woman," or we read real books. Television was rarely on until evening. We only had the two channels anyway, St. Louis and Memphis, with only a handful of shows like "Dragnet" or wrestling, and everything was in black and white.

HALLOWEEN

Halloween was fun. We kids would take off and roam the neighborhoods with our pillowcases to haul in the candy. We didn't have special costumes. Everyone made their own—usually witches, hoboes, princesses, or cowboys. Store-bought costumes weren't available, and we couldn't have afforded them if they were. Sometimes parents wanted to show off their creativity in the costuming. We were free to go pretty much wherever we wished. No one worried about crime, because it just didn't exist back then in our area. It could be scary though, on some of the poorly lit back streets. Our imaginations were the only source of any real fear.

SUMMERTIME

Every summer, we left our doors and windows open because we didn't have air-conditioning. It didn't matter how hot it got. We were used to it because of all the time spent working outside in extreme heat. The farm pond was always a welcome sight. We had window fans to draw the cool air in at night. (It also drew in all of the barnyard dust.) We would often sit under that big elm tree in the evenings until the temperature cooled down. Once in a while, if we were lucky, we might even get a "sodie pop."

SPECIAL SATURDAY OUTINGS

I remember vividly the Anna drive-in theater (located where the Walmart now sits). There were no other businesses nearby—just a large open area for the drive-in. It was a great place to see wonderful old black and white movies. We would grab pillows and lay on top of the cars. People brought lawn chairs if they wanted to sit outside their cars. There was a concession stand for drinks, popcorn, and candy. Many would bring their own snacks from home. It was common to see cars packed full of kids. Sometimes, kids would even be hidden in the trunk. Since there was a flat charge per vehicle, the more kids, the cheaper the price. Concession stands were for those with money—or someone trying to impress their date. There aren't many drive-ins left, but they sure provided lots of entertainment for us as kids.

MORE OBSERVATIONS

I could go on and on about the '40s, '50s, and '60s. Values were strong back then. Divorce was rare. Crime was low. When my dad was Union County Sheriff from 1963-66, he had only one deputy. Three or four Illinois State Troopers were also at Dad's disposal. In 2018, the number of deputies and State Police is much larger, due to the increase in drugs and other crimes.

Everyone who was a little brother or sister wore hand-me-downs. Our tennis shoes didn't have name brands or player endorsements, except for the Chuck Taylor shoe. The shoes I wore were purchased at P.N. Hirsh. When they got dirty, Mom would wash them, and when they were dry, we would put white shoe polish on them. (Converse "Chuck Taylor" shoes are still popular.)

Everyone who went to public school had to be vaccinated, unless they could provide proof of vaccination. Childhood diseases like polio, measles, and chicken pox were still common. We stood in long lines to get our shots. The size of those needles was frightening. The longer we stood in line smelling the alcohol, the more we thought about sneaking out. One boy did just that. He lived close to school, and the principal quickly apprehended him. Getting the polio shot was a different story. No one minded getting the polio vaccine because it was administered in a sugar cube. We all knew about the "Iron Lung" machine, and no one wanted to end up in one of those. (I can still see images of those old machines in my mind.) Polio was wiped out in the late '50s when Dr. Jonas Salk introduced the Salk vaccine.

Chapter 6

More Observations about Cultural Change

ENTITLEMENT

Most boys in the '40s and '50s joined sports teams. When I played for the Jonesboro Bulldogs, there weren't any female teams. Title IX wasn't established until around 1975. While I was coaching in Jonesboro, we started our first female basketball and softball programs.

We only had basketball and track when I was in high school. Softball was a physical education sport. We didn't have four or five team sports a year. And if we played, we were responsible for getting to and from practice. Kids in town could ride their bikes or walk, but it was a little more trouble for those of us who lived on the farm.

Today, many people believe in "entitlement." For example, some schools give ribbons or trophies to everyone, just for participation. I don't agree with this. My philosophy over the years has been to encourage athletes to earn a trophy through hard work. Just showing up is expected. Falling short in a sporting event prepares a person for the disappointment that will happen if he or she doesn't work hard. I don't want them to get the idea that just showing up is ok. I want them to develop discipline and a good work ethic that will produce positive results. If a student athlete falls short, we'll go back and work on getting better. Goal-setting contributes to success. Ask any athlete why he or she succeeded, and they will tell you it was because of goal-setting and hard work. Set some goals. Figure out what you are good at and what you enjoy most. Believe you can achieve your goals. Never give up. Involve others to assist. These ideals are essential for success in sports and in a career. I have seen it prove true in many of my student athletes, as they have grown up. Many of them have made me so proud, because they have gone on to excel in their careers. Those who have potential and fail to use their God-given talents and potential are dying with music still left in them.

Fans in the '40s and '50s

We witnessed very little unsportsmanlike conduct in the '50s. Parents were not always able to attend games. It was nice that my mom usually got to come, but Dad was usually still working, Sometimes, even Mom missed because she was busy cooking or canning. Also, only the winning team would get a trophy. Second and third place teams might get ribbons.

When we won the Olive Branch Invitational defeating Shawnee in 1953, I think it was the first team trophy of my career at Jonesboro. The excitement was great. (Olive Branch school was torn down many years ago. The school is in the Egyptian school district now.) That gym was so small, but to us it seemed a large arena. It was instilled in us by Coach Alcorn and Coach Hartline that sportsmanship was a priority. (I do remember Coach Alcorn getting red as a beet, but he never lost control. I was privileged to get to teach with him in 1979 at the Anna-Jonesboro Community High School.) When I played freshman football, he would get excited and send the wrong kid into the game or call a player by the wrong name. It was comical at times, but I always respected him. I once wrote a letter to the editor of the paper about what a wonderful role model and Christian man he was. I attended church with him at the First Christian Church in Anna.

DISCIPLINE

Teachers were allowed to discipline children and classrooms were quiet. I occupied classrooms in the '50s and taught in the '60s and '70s. Discipline was still strong into the late '70s, but then came the removal of the paddle. I now teach physical education at Lick Creek Elementary. By todays standards, we have fairly good discipline, however, it's a far cry from the early days of classroom control. I have always said there can be very little learning without discipline. I have even been called a "boot camp drill instructor" by some parents. I always say, "Thank you." My classes are very structured. That is the only way I will teach. If we worry about what others think, we will water down our curriculum. It's the same with coaching. There can only be one head coach. If a teacher or coach starts to listen to every parent or fan, their philosophy will be greatly altered. I used to say to angry parents, "There's the door if you don't like what I'm doing with your kid." I will emphatically say that most of the Lick Creek parents have always been very respectful of what I'm doing.

My dad always seemed to know when I got into trouble at school. I think he had a hot line to the principal's desk. I knew that the belt would come out as soon as he found out that I was in trouble at school. At the time, I didn't realize that Dad was good friends with Mr. R.C Martin, the principal. It also didn't help to have my aunt as a 6th grade teacher. I couldn't move without her watching me. I may have even been a little paranoid about her telling Dad. What she did was make me think she had talked to Dad. She certainly didn't need any help.

There's a popular saying, "One bad apple will spoil the whole apple crate." We, however, are reluctant to follow through with this counsel, whether in the classroom or on the athletic field. A problem then has the potential to disrupt a whole classroom or team. As a result, we create a much larger problem. Teachers, administrators, and coaches are not allowed to administer discipline as they were 50 years ago. Lawsuits abound, and many times, parents support their own children instead of backing the faculty or staff. Sixty-five years ago, when we got in trouble at school, it meant we were also in trouble at home.

My high school coach Bennie Purcell was a strong disciplinarian. I have great respect for Coach Purcell for the discipline he taught me. Our parents are now deceased, and so is Coach Purcell, but Donnie Ray, Tony Ferrell, Don Denny, Jim Shepherd, or Steve Tweedy can verify the following stories as true.

The first story involved our game with the Pinckneyville Panthers—a top-rated program in the state of Illinois year in and year out. The year was 1958. We lost to the Panthers by 30 points.

We stunk up the AJ gym that night. The game was over by 9:30 p.m. Coach Purcell said, "Go down to the locker room and change into your practice gear; we are going to practice." We didn't question him. My parents sat at the top of the bleachers along with the other parents until our extended practice was over. If there were any complaints from anyone, I was never aware of it.

If we gave up the baseline as so many players do today, our punishment was four swats with a paddle. We had to bend over the stage wall where we received our "fundamental of the game adjustment." Ask Don Denny, he will tell you the same thing.

Another illustration of old-school discipline is the time Coach Purcell took the entire starting five down to the locker room while the game was still in progress. I had already graduated but was in attendance. He left his assistant coach in charge of the rest of the team. I assume he gave the team an "attitude adjustment." That was the only time I ever saw anything like that during a game.

The outstanding coach was definitely "old school," but he had a lot of success at Anna-Jonesboro and Mt. Vernon High Schools. At the collegiate level, he won many

Ohio Valley Conference titles in tennis. He was inducted into the Murray State Hall of Fame a few years ago.

INTERACTION

In many ways, it was the best of times because people had been through hard times together. We had to make the best of what we had. That led to the satisfaction of accomplishment through hard work. Most people were self-disciplined and hard workers. There weren't many "couch potatoes." People actually looked at each other as they talked with one another—no texting or staring at iPads or iPhones; no wasted time glued to computer screens or video games. These devices can be useful; however, they can become an obsession, especially with young people. I'm thankful for those parents who control the use of these devices.

DRAMATIC CULTURAL CHANGE

More families prayed together and stayed together back in the '40s and '50s. They provided their own food with their gardens, cleaned up their own messes, took responsibility for their actions, had pride in ownership, and found many ways to entertain themselves, often by simply going outdoors.

How different even everyday objects were back in the '50s. From school supplies to automobiles and other means of transportation, things have changed dramatically. We used pencils and ink pens filled from an ink jar. The ink pens were messy and tempting for little boys sitting behind little girls with pigtails. Often, the ink spilled, and it was very difficult to remove from clothing or from the wooden desk. Pencils were cleaner and used very effectively in most schools. Bic finally came out with an affordable pen that became very popular in the late '50s. Many of our reports were done on old black Remington typewriters with carriage returns. However, if mistakes were made, you couldn't erase or hit "backspace" like you can on a computer. Errors had to be corrected with WiteOut or white correction tape. It was very time consuming.

Toy cars were made from steel with rubber wheels. Mom's doctor was Roy Keith, MD, whose office was upstairs over the old E.P. Owen Drugstore at the four-way across from what is now the Anna State Bank. Dr. Keith had steel toy trucks, cars, and tractors which I was fascinated with. We never had wind-up cars like those because they were cost-prohibitive. There was no such thing then as remote- controlled cars or trucks. We didn't even have battery-operated ones.

We did enjoy gluing balsa wood airplanes together. You could buy them in a little kit at P.N. Hirsh or the 5&10 dime store. They would fly, but not very well. The wind had to be just right.

THE CADILLAC AMBULANCE

An old Cadillac ambulance was used for funerals and emergencies. It was a large all-metal (no plastic bumpers) vehicle that seemed like it had to weigh ten tons.

The hearse is only used for funeral services now, because we have the Union County ambulance service which uses state-of-the-art medical equipment to handle emergency situations. Many years ago, however, it was the funeral homes that handled most of the emergencies.

IRON STEAM ENGINES

We had a 30-acre field located right along Route 127, three miles south of Jonesboro. The railroad used steam engines at the time, and they were fascinating to watch as they went by. I always liked to wave at the engineer, and they would almost always wave back. They knew the thrill kids would get watching them chug along. Locomotives had large "cow catchers" located low on the front. In case of a collision with an animal, it could push it off to the side.

SCHOOL BOOKS

My teacher in first grade was Mrs. Mabel Manees. I remember my first introduction to Dick and Jane. I learned to read with many of the old basic books and stories. "See Dick and Jane run. See Puff run. See Dick run. See Jane run. Run, run, run." We learned to read with those simple but effective books.

THE MAYTAG WASHING MACHINE

Mom's old Maytag washing machine was located in the basement with a vent hose going out the window to dispose of the fumes from the gas- burning engine. There was no dryer, so clothes were wrung out by the attachment on the top of the washer. It had two rollers. The clothes would be inserted through the wringers to squeeze out the water, then hung on the clothesline to dry. New cotton clothing would have to be bought one size too large because it would shrink. Washing was a major chore every week. One of the students at school was hurt

when he got his arm caught in the rollers and bruised pretty badly. After the clothes were dried, they would need to be ironed. Since we didn't have a steam iron, Mom used a bottle with holes in the lid to sprinkle them. Annie Meisenheimer was very conservative with her cistern water, so she would hang her clothes out on the clothesline the night before she was to iron. The dew would wet the clothes enough for her to iron the next morning. Now you get an idea of how she and Doug could save such a large amount of money in their lifetime. (I wonder if she ever had any bird stains on Arley's bed sheets.)

OLD SEWING MACHINES

Most of the old sewing machines had to be pumped by foot. I remember some of our neighbors using them, but I don't remember if Mom had one. I do know that, when the sewing was completed, the sewing machine would fold down underneath the table so it could be used as a regular table. Many homes had them because it was cost-prohibitive to buy lots of garments like pants or shirts. And it made patching garments a lot easier than doing it by hand.

BY-GONE SOCIAL ISSUES

Almost no shops were open on Sundays in the rural areas of Southern Illinois or Southeast Missouri back in the '40s and '50s. Malls hadn't been thought of yet. Today, with malls in every city, Sunday is a busy shopping day. In my home town, many businesses still close on Sunday. One of the reasons for "blue laws" was the fact that many people attended church on Sunday, and it was supposed to be a day of rest.

TEACHERS

In rural America, teachers were treated with respect for the most part. I can't answer whether this was the case in cities. If the movie *Grease* is accurate, teachers in cities had their hands full, even back in the '50s. The main offenses our teachers faced were talking back, spit wads, getting out of line, and chewing gum. Drugs weren't even relevant. Teachers were held in high esteem. To this day, I can still name all of my teachers. I especially remember the ones who were the hardest on me. Many years later, I apologized to some of them for my bad behavior. Maybe that's why I'm strict with my physical education classes now.

WATER GUNS

Water guns used to be allowed in school, and our teachers were pretty tolerant of them, if used appropriately. There was to be no ganging up on each other or soaking a student. A student walking into school today with a water gun would be in serious trouble. There have been so many school shootings that anything that resembles a gun in school is cause for concern.

"Happy Hour"

I love my kids and want them to be good citizens. I know that was the case with the teachers who were hardest on me. They told me so. Sometimes, kids will defend the teacher's discipline and even chastise some of the other kids for misbehaving. At Lick Creek, I have many kids in physical education who will tell the unruly kids to get their act together.

Recently I got news that the fourth and fifth graders were showing disrespect to their teachers. They were also trying to talk over me during instruction time in physical education class. I decided to take a couple of class days to discuss respecting others. I spent a lot of time talking about manners and courteousness and the importance of saying "Thank you; Please; You're welcome; Excuse me; Yes, ma'am; and No, sir."

They seemed to catch on about the value of respect. However, before a full day passed, I got reports of disrespect running rampant. I was furious. When they came into the gym, I said, "Spread out all over the gym floor. We are going to have a "Happy Hour." I learned about "Happy Hour" during my Great Lakes Basic Training Camp days. The training center was in Great Lakes, Illinois. We had them quite often when we messed up marching or did something stupid in front of our commanding officer. They were looking for any reason to discipline us. The "Happy Hour" was one hour of physical fitness. It included planks, sit- ups, leg raises, isometric push-ups, sprints, jumping jacks, side-straddle hops, and many other fitness skills I have chosen to forget. Since our physical education classes are only 40 minutes, our "Happy Hour" was shorter, but the "attitude adjustment" worked wonders. Now, I hear more "Good morning; Thanks; You're welcome"; and even "Have a good evening, Coach Ron."

Another thing the kids didn't think about was walking between people who are talking. They rarely said, "Excuse me." In the lunch room Sherri Houseman and Mrs. Alsip now have them saying, "Thank you; Please; and Yes, ma'am." We all work together at Lick Creek to teach the students good manners and respect. Things are so different today because kids witness so much disrespect on TV. Politicians set a terrible example for our youth when they name call. Many kids have been taught respect at home, and it's a pleasure to behold. Our jobs as parents, teachers, and coaches is to help make good citizens out of our kids. We are committed to teaching core requirements and respect for authority and helping them grow up into responsible adults.

PREGNANCY

Pregnant girls were a rarity in the '50s. If someone became pregnant, she was soon gone from school. I remember one in my graduating class who left school and never returned to graduate. Many times, the reason a girl left school was concealed, and some other excuse was made. Most never returned to the school they left. It was a real stigma. Society was very unforgiving at the time towards anyone who got pregnant "out of wedlock." Our current climate is more forgiving and has a completely different attitude toward pregnancy. Out of wedlock pregnancies are much more prevalent today. Youth are exposed to so much more sexual content than in previous years. Many pregnancy centers now exist in Southern Illinois and Southeast Missouri to provide assistance to unwed mothers. In the '50s, pregnancy centers were not available, and fingers were pointed. Low-income families and families with alcoholism were often blamed. A last name might be whispered, and someone would say, "I'm not surprised." Society was quick to judge, but today, pregnancies are seen in every socio-economic class, and the finger-pointing has ceased.

RACE RELATIONS

We were so ignorant about the black population when I was in grade school and high school. Jokes about blacks were told out of pure ignorance. I was in the Navy in 1966 before I ever really got to know any black people. My wife and I befriended a black couple while stationed at the Naval Torpedo Station in Keyport, Washington. We became great friends, and they would babysit for us on occasion. Some of my best friends today are African-Americans. Two who have been good friends to Paula and me are Willie Smith and Bob Love. Both are successful athletes; Willie is an Olympic Gold Medalist, and Bob is a four-time NBA basketball player for the Chicago Bulls. Both conducted many camps with me over the past 25 years. Willie and Bob have each shared stories about how hard it was growing up in the '40s and '50s. Jonesboro didn't have any black residents, to my knowledge. Dad did hire some black workers from the Mounds area to pick green beans, once. I was never around any of them. My blood boils if I ever hear the N-word used, and I will quickly react with a strong reprimand.

Willie Smith

DARE TO DREAM

While I was working with Bob (Butterbean) Love, I discovered that his growing up years were like ours in many ways. The only difference was that Bruce and I made $12 a day and Bob only made $2 a day. We were picking corn, and Bob was picking cotton on the plantation they lived on. A boy asked me once if Bob was a slave. No, he wasn't, but he did live on the O'Neil plantation in Delhi, Louisiana, in 1942. He was born many years after slavery. Bob's family didn't have running water or any T.V. They were poor, but, like us, they didn't recognize it. Like myself, he played many make-believe basketball games against the side of his Grandma's old house. He dreamed he was playing against Oscar Robertson, Bill

Russell, Wilt Chamberlain, Jerry West, Bob Petit, and other great basketball players just like I did. I had a bicycle rim and a basketball with a bladder in it. It was not round like today's basketballs. Bob played against the side of his Grandma's old house; his rim was a coat hanger, and his ball was a bag stuffed with grass, paper, and socks. That led me to believe Bob was much poorer than our family. He, like me, imagined winning many games on last second shots. The big difference between my dreams and Bob's dreams was huge. He actually played against every one of the players he dreamed about. I only got to meet a few of them.

Bob Love, Chicago Bulls; Myself; Walter White, Kansas City Chiefs

Myself; Bob Love, Chicago Bulls; Edward M. Smith, President of Union Labor Life Insurance Company in our recreation room in Jonesboro.

Bob Love, Chicago Bulls; Jerry Sloan, Chicago Bulls & Utah Jazz; Doug Collins, Philadelphia 76ers; NBA Sports Analyst and former Bulls trainer.

STYLE CHANGES

We always wore bib overalls or blue Levi jeans with a white T-shirt to school. The girls wore pleated skirts with bobby socks and penny loafers. The movie *Grease* portrays the 50s pretty accurately. The rebel boys wore greasy hairdos like "the Fonz" from the television show "Happy Days." Crew cuts were popular, too. My coach Bennie Purcell required us to wear crew cuts during basketball season. My friend Rich Herrin also required crew cuts for basketball. That was part of the discipline in the 50s. Today, you are likely to see ponytails on the court or hair hanging down over the player's eyes.

Men wore brim hats to just about every event. Men attended church wearing brim hats and a suit. The hats were also a common sight at sporting events. When Rick Livesay asked me what it was like attending the 1908 Chicago Cubs World Series game, I told him we wore our brim straw hats with a suit and tie. (I wasn't really at that game, of course!) Women wore colorful hats and white gloves, especially to church. It was amusing during the Easter services to try to see over those large hats. In fact, it was rare to see a woman in church without a hat.

We didn't have much of a clue about apparel worn in other cultures. Social media was nonexistent. We never saw an Indian, Italian, Polish, Russian, Chinese, or any other ethnic group outside of movies. It was a little more common to see a Japanese person because of the news reels of the Pearl Harbor attack, or of the Japanese encampments in the U.S.

FAMILY SIZE IN RURAL AREAS

Many families had anywhere from eight to nineteen kids, right here in Union County. It wasn't uncommon for families in rural areas to have lots of children. In fact, it was often considered an advantage. The older children would assist with raising the younger children. I remember a Union County family with 15 children. That family had plenty of help with their "truck cropping" (small patch cropping). They raised cucumbers, squash, tomatoes, peppers, and strawberries. When Dad went out of the peach-growing business in the 40s, we had about 150 dozen peach baskets leftover. That family purchased all those baskets for their farm operation, paying on a weekly basis until they were paid for.

Having a baby in the 30s and 40s was not a major medical expense like it is today. It seems unbelievable now that anyone could afford to have so many children. Birth control was rare. Today, the high cost of raising a child to adulthood makes large families the exception rather than the rule. Raising a child through the college years can cost hundreds of thousands of dollars. But back in rural America in the '40s, life was simpler. People lived mainly off of their land. Food was eaten fresh or canned. In large families, the children remained on the farm and assisted in working the land, as well as harvesting the crops. The family who purchased our peach baskets lived very well. Their labor force was their children.

Chapter 7

My Education

MY TEACHERS AT JONESBORO GRADE SCHOOL (1947-1955)

Most of my teachers had a tremendous influence on me. We were raised to show respect to all of our teachers. My first-grade teacher was Mrs. Manees, who in later years was my mom's nextdoor neighbor. My second-grade teacher was the principal's wife, Mrs. Martin. Mrs. R.C. Martin was a very good teacher. My third-grade teacher was Mrs. Glascock, whom I don't remember well. She was already up in years when I had her.

My fourth-grade teacher, Mrs. Pauline Clark, was very tough and demanding. I feel I learned the most from her. Fourth grade is a very critical year for learning many of the basics. She drilled us in everything—multiplication tables, reading, writing, and spelling. One of the main things I learned, which I'm still proud of today, is penmanship. We drilled over and over on the Palmer method of writing. That curriculum is no longer taught, and it shows in the quality of kids' writing. To this day, I still know my multiplication tables and have always been a pretty good speller. My fifth-grade teacher, Mrs. Vaughn, was firm, fair, and an excellent teacher, especially in geography, social studies, and civics. We learned the states and the capitals. I still remember most of them. Fortunately, I have been to over 40 states and in 25 or more capitals during the time I sold insurance and while I was with the Laborers' International Union.

My sixth-grade teacher, Mrs. Zada Foehr, was my dad's sister and one of the toughest teachers I ever had. I couldn't get by with anything. I was small for my age and would do things to attract attention. She rode me hard. If I belched or did something else to attract attention, she was on my case before a second passed. "I may have to talk with your dad," she'd say. She never talked to him; it was a bluff, and it worked very well. She broke me early in the first semester. Over 65 years later, I was talking with some good friends in the Lick Creek area. The two gentlemen were talking about how mean their teacher was at their one-room school. They showed me a picture of their class and pointed out the teacher. It was my Aunt Zada Foehr! I said, "Shame on both of you for talking about my Aunt Zada like that." We laughed. Those two men were Morris (Moose) Hall and Glad Hall. Now I have Moose's grandkids in school at Lick Creek.

My seventh-grade teacher was Mrs. Bertha Hunsaker. God bless her. She had a terrible time with discipline. Her name was Bertha, and the kids liked to call her "Birtie." Someone in a crowd of kids would call out, "Birtie, Birtie, Birtie" either at school or up town around the Twins Cafe.

Once, I tried it, but Mom and Dad put an end to that. They said, "If we hear of any more disrespectful antics out of you on this matter, you will be dealt with harshly." I'm not proud of what I did, and I'm not making an excuse. However, she just didn't know how to display the right kind of discipline. She should have worn our buttocks out. We never would have done something like that to Mrs. Foehr. Mrs. Hunsaker would yell at us and say she was going to call the sheriff. It was her responsibility to handle problems, not the sheriff's. Anyway, I don't know of a sheriff that would touch a situation like that. Years later, I saw her and apologized for my behavior. I said, "Mrs. Hunsacker, I wished you would have put a paddle to our buttocks!" She was a sweet lady, but she was way too easy on us. John Rosemond, who wrote *Parenting by the Book*, said the teachers he remembers best are the ones who were the hardest on him. Same with me.

My eighth-grade teacher was Mrs. Greer. I will never forget her. She was as tough, or even tougher than my Aunt Zada. When she entered the room, we would snap into place—somewhat like we did with my company commander at Great Lakes Training Center in Great Lakes, Illinois! She rarely smiled, and that was to let everyone know she was in control. Boy! Was she ever in control! We learned so much, as a result of her discipline. Like I've said to so many young teachers, including my own granddaughter, Ms. Walter, who is our new fifth-grade teacher at Lick Creek Elementary, "Don't smile until Christmas." Quoting John Rosemond again, "People raised in the 1950s have difficulty relating to the new parenting norm because our parents were the center of our attention, not the other way around." In my classrooms, I see so much excuse-making when the work becomes difficult. People are supposed to develop coping skills when necessary, not use an excuse every time they don't meet with a certain level of success. The students in my physical education classes who are excelling are the ones who develop a good work ethic. I can, with certainty, after nearly fifty years of working with youth, predict whether parents have been "parenting by the book." The Bible is a great parenting book. Compare the number of young people today who are depressed or are taking prescription drugs to the number in the 1940s and 1950s. In my opinion, kids have way too much idle time, too little responsibility, and too few opportunities for commitment. John Rosemond says, "The most character-building word is the two-letter word: 'NO'."

One other person who was a big influence on my life was my principal, Mr. R.C. Martin, at Jonesboro Grade School. One didn't want any part of going to his office. Some of the teachers preferred sending students to the office over paddling themselves. Mr. Martin had an effective way of talking to kids and making them understand that what they had done was not acceptable. He rarely had to use the paddle. He was very convincing when he said, "I'd better not see you back in here. The next time won't be pleasant for you." It almost always worked!

My first three music teachers were Ms. Brown, Ms. White, and Ms. Gray (all color names). I saw Ms. Brown in 2013 in Dongola, and we talked about those early days at Jonesboro Grade School. She was one of the best band teachers I've ever known. She taught at Dongola and also at Cobden for several years. Her marching bands still stand out in my mind. Bands today rarely wear uniforms. The bands she instructed were neatly dressed in uniforms, and lines were straight. She herself was dressed in a neat band uniform as she marched alongside the band. I admired her then, and I respect her even more today. What an impact she had on many, many students. I imagine many went to college on band scholarships. Years later, I interviewed her for my first book. She's in her 90s now.

As I mentioned earlier, one should never have an aunt for their teacher. I got a kick out of Glad and Moose Hall talking about how mean she was. Years later, we realize that "mean" just meant effective discipline. They attended Sitter School when she was "mean to" (disciplined) them. I know them well enough to know they probably earned everything that they got. Glad told me about the time he took lizards into the school. Moose verified the incident, which tells me he had a part in it. The lizards were stuffed in Glad's pockets as he entered the one-room school. They all got loose and scattered all over the school house floor! The teacher told Glad to go get a switch, so he did. He brought back a skinny little straw-like switch. She said, "Go back and get something that I can whip you with." The next time, he brought a huge piece of wood larger than a fence post. It was so wet and heavy he struggled to get it into the classroom.

Zada D. Fulenwider
(Mrs. Fred M. Foehr)
8–6–1892 –

109

That made the teacher furious! She said, "I'll go get one myself." She came with a perfect-size switch and wore him out. It was a whipping he, to this day, has not forgotten.

I remember being scared to death of Mr. Rodenbeck, one of the 8th grade teachers. Once, I had to go upstairs to his classroom when I was only a 2nd or 3rd grader. Another student and I had done something wrong, and we had to meet with him. The desks seemed huge, and so was Mr. Rodenbeck. We thought everything was huge. I'm sure the teacher who sent us upstairs knew that it would be intimidating. It was, and we didn't have to go upstairs anymore. Fortunately, I didn't have to have Mr. Rodenbeck, because he was gone by the time I arrived in junior high.

THE CRAWL SPACE

One day, as 8th graders, we decided to explore the crawi space under the Jonesboro school. We had some free time (maybe recess), so we decided to sneak into the opening to explore the space under the school and get back out before anyone would know. We were wrong! Mr. Hartline was waiting on us as we exited the crawl space into the shop area. We each received a good old-fashioned rear-end warming. Our poor judgment (stupidity) got us exactly what we deserved. That was the end of our exploring days at the school.

School Closings and Earlier Teachers

My friends Larry Morgan and Richard Reynolds didn't attend Jonesboro school until their 4th or 5th grade years. It seemed odd because Larry and Richard lived only two or three miles from me in the McClure school district not far from the Berryville area of west Jonesboro. I lived off the Old Cape Road. McClure school stayed in session longer than the Lake Hill School, for some reason. Maybe their township was financially sounder than ours. By the early 50s, most of the one-room schools were closed. (My Aunt Zada had taught at Lyerla and Sitter schools before teaching in Jonesboro around 1950.)

All my teachers were very professional except for a few. They demanded our attention and got it, most of the time. We studied the basic subjects of reading, writing, and arithmetic—the 3Rs. We had civics and studied geography. We were drilled heavily in all of our subjects. We learned all the states, the capitals, and the multiplication tables, and I still remember them. We didn't have calculators and computers or other modern devices. I believe our society as a whole may have lost some problem-solving and creative thinking abilities as a result. Once, at a fast food restaurant, the cash register malfunctioned. The cashier couldn't calculate the simplest return of my change.

MISBEHAVIOR AT SCHOOL

The major infractions in classrooms in the 1950s were shooting paper wads, chewing gum, getting out of line, water guns, marbles, and pigtails dipped in ink wells on the desks. Today, sadly, the problems are drugs, alcohol, guns, pregnancies, and disrespect for authority. At Lick Creek, where I teach now, I still see evidence of the same kind of moral fiber as the 50s. We have some incredible parents who are involved with the school and their children's activities. I have never seen a community like Lick Creek. Even so, it's not perfect, and some parents can be difficult.

I don't use the paddle anymore, but I do have a method called "Happy Hour" that is very effective. Nationwide, we are seeing a major breakdown in our moral compass. Disrespect is widespread. Manners are also showing a decline. At Lick Creek School we work hard at addressing these problems.

Back in the 50s, we had a few class clowns, me being one. Kids showed disrespect to others at times, but rarely to a teacher or staff person. We knew that disrespect to a teacher or staff member would result in the board of education (paddle).

Kids can be cruel at times. We had some classmates who were overweight, and kids would make fun of them. It was rare to see a kid who was overweight in the 40s and 50s, so they became targets of cruel and thoughtless remarks. Today, childhood obesity is common. Maybe it's because there were no fast food establishments. We only had the Twins Cafe and the Dixie BBQ, which is still in business today. It looks the same except for the extension on the west side. Even the wooden seats are the same. I remember George Ferguson making them. George and Bea Ferguson built the Dixie in 1947 and owned it for many years. Mom and Dad were very good friends with the Fergusons. They fished together, mainly at Horseshoe Lake in Olive Branch, Illinois. George was an avid fisherman. Dad fished when he could. Farming usually kept him pretty busy.

My High School Years - Athletics

My high school experience started slowly and ended on a very high note. 1955 was the beginning of a totally new experience in my education, as I was pretty scared to go to a much larger school. I didn't know many kids besides my classmates at Jonesboro. I did know a few kids from Anna and Lick Creek through 4-H, but I was still small for my age and very shy. I was one of those kids who would say, "I hope the teacher doesn't call on me." I was very self-conscious about my size. I stood 5' 1" as an incoming freshman and weighed 96 pounds. There were a few more kids my size like Jerry Hines, Mike Keller, and Richard Diefenbach. But I did get to play football. I was a specialist. Not many incoming freshmen got to do what I did. Coach Abernathy and Coach Alcorn saw a talent in me. They assigned me to hold the dummies for the varsity. Two players named John Chamness and John (Butch) Sneddon, each weighing around 200 pounds, brought me down many times. They would take the dummy down along with me. (I think there might have been two dummies.) The uniform didn't fit properly, which frustrated me. They didn't have a uniform small enough for me. We would have to tape our thigh pads on our legs so they wouldn't move around. I got issued the outdated old leather helmet. I felt like a dork! Kids today would laugh if they ever saw me in my football gear. I was not an All-State football player in the making! The other freshmen were also issued the leather helmets. At least, I wasn't the only one. The varsity got the cool, updated helmets.

Running in those very uncomfortable uniforms with the thigh pads taped was a chore. Coach Alcorn would beat me in the sprints. He would dress out in his hip pads and football pants. I knew I was not the fastest freshman on the team. Richard Diefenbach, Jerry Hines, and I finished close to last most of the time. Those thigh pads were awful. We used them as our excuse. As I have said many times as a coach, "Any old excuse will do when you need one." Well, we needed more than one. We were little and slow. We had some juniors and seniors who were very fast. Bill Lewis and Bill Pitts were very fast and outstanding players, too.

Coach Alcorn taught us how to block and tackle. I was always impressed with his speed. He always ran a sprint or two with us. He played football at Cape State (SEMO University) in the 40s. Mike Keller was small but became one of the finest football players in the history of Anna-Jonesboro. What made him great was his mental toughness and aggressiveness. The movie "Rudy" reminded me of Mike. He only weighed around 140 pounds, but after every tackle (and he made a lot of them), he would bounce right back up ready for the next play. Pound for pound, I have never seen a tougher player. Kevin Jung, who played years later, reminded me of Mike. Richard Diefenbach played all four years and grew into an enormous 145 pounds. He was small but also a good player. He had heart. I played my freshman and sophomore years but was unable to continue my junior year as I was needed on the farm to help my father with chores and the farming operations. My football career was a tough two years; I practiced every day. Dad said, "If you start something, you finish it." I don't remember ever missing a practice. I finally did start growing and was 5' 9" my junior year and about 140 pounds.

Under Coach Halter, we won the conference both our freshman and sophomore years. Our freshman team went undefeated. It was the first time the freshman team had won the conference crown in school history.

HIGH SCHOOL TEACHERS

I was privileged to have some fine teachers at Anna-Jonesboro, just as I'd had at Jonesboro Grade School. Ella Jane Pickles Sanders was my English teacher. She'd taught my dad and his sisters. She was as tough as nails. She graded all test papers in green ink and had beautiful penmanship. She taught for over 50 years and appeared on the Gary Moore show "I've Got a Secret." Her secret was that she'd taught four generations of students. Those students appeared on the show with her.

She had failed my dad and some of his sisters, so I was dreading the class. I made it through the class with a C- average. I did fail one semester, so I brought a nine-pound turnip to her. She kept it on her desk for several days and seemed to enjoy having it. The next semester my grade came up to a C+. I honestly did do better. I don't think the turnip helped, or did it? She and Mrs. Bartow had a building named after them—Bar-San Hall.

Mr. Alcorn was the driver education, history, and safety teacher. Driver education didn't start until the '60s, so I didn't have him for that. I really admired Mr. Alcorn because of his honesty and integrity. I did see him get mad at grade school basketball and football games. He would get as red as a beet, but never lost control. Years later, while working on the same faculty, I discovered he was a real cut-up. He once went into the coach's office and placed plastic soap in the coach's shower. Larry Miles, a good friend of mine, who was in Mr. Alcorn's driver education class, told this story. Often, the route took them out Route 146 to I-57. They would drive north a while, then return to school. One particular day Mr. Alcorn fell asleep, and his students didn't wake him. They just continued to drive. They ended up in Salem, 110 miles north, by the time Mr. Alcorn woke up.

Don Skelton shared another driver education story. It was test day at the end of the semester, so class times were extended. They were in a red 4-door Chevy Caprice—maybe a 1976 model from Coad Chevrolet. Another student, Jim Zimmerman, and Don were driving on the Old Cape Road near Route 3 when Mr. Alcorn realized that the students might be late for the next class. Jim Zimmerman was driving. He told Jim to step on it. Jim complied and drove a lot faster than had ever been allowed prior. Don was in the back seat, and Jim came up on one of those old one-lane raised bridges, and he did not slow down at all. It felt like they were airborne as they came off the bridge. Jim looked at Don in the mirror and grinned real big. Mr. Alcorn never said a word, except to remind Jim to hurry! It wasn't long before they sped through another one-lane bridge and had the same exhilarating experience. Jim loved the opportunity to speed back to school, and neither of the guys can remember if they made it back to school on time.

Don also remembered that, on a few occasions, Mr. Alcorn would have them drive to Saratoga Park so he could drink some "togy" water—no one else would try the water since it smelled like rotten eggs.

Mr. Alcorn was especially good to the Skelton family. He would take them to St. Louis to see the Cardinals play, and they would go to the zoo. Don's parents were both blind and didn't own a car, and Mr. Alcorn didn't want the kids to miss out on fun experiences. He always volunteered his time and paid for all of the activities. He was wonderful, caring person.

Mr. Dodd, my chemistry teacher, was my dad's childhood friend. Our families would get together quite often in the summer months for ice cream socials. Mr. Dodd also worked for Dad taking in hay. Because of the friendship, I thought it would be great having Mr. Dodd. I decided to take chemistry thinking I would get preferential treatment. I was wrong. He was tough but fair. I wasn't treated any differently than any of the other students. That is the way it is supposed to be. I found out that chemistry was fun. I was pretty good at doing chemical equations and enjoyed the lab experiments. That might have affected my decision to minor in science at Southeast Missouri State University.

Mrs. Grace Odum was my sophomore English teacher. She was an outstanding teacher who demanded absolute total attention to the subject at hand. She had zero tolerance for goofing off. She gave me many detentions for inattention. My dad found out that I had been giving her trouble. I will never forget what Dad told me in front of Mom, "I'm going to remove you from school because it's quite obvious that you aren't there to learn. I'm in need of help here on the farm." That hit me like a ton of bricks! I didn't want to be taken out of school. I had so many friends whom I would miss. I loved physical education and playing basketball, and it would be really lonesome on the farm. That was my sophomore year, and I never got another detention the rest of my high school career. I had one more English class under Mrs. Odum, and I did well. By the time I graduated high school, she and I had developed a deep respect for one another.

Mr. O.K. Loomis was the agriculture teacher at AJ. I loved agriculture and being in the F.F.A. Mr. Loomis taught just about everything a farm boy would love. We studied animal husbandry, forage and fiber crops, welding, judging cattle, hogs, sheep, and grain crops. Since we raised sheep, cattle, and hogs, it was wonderful to study the different breeds of animals. I took some agriculture courses at Southeast Missouri State, since I enjoyed them so much in high school. That is a tribute to Mr. Dodd and Mr. Loomis for making the curriculum interesting.

Mr. Otto Ohmart, my biology teacher, was a very good science teacher. He made it interesting by doing so many fascinating experiments and dissections of animals. His delight in the subject was contagious. Because he also was such a great teacher, I took courses at Southeast

118

Missouri State in biology, zoology, anatomy, microbiology, bacteriology and even Physiology of Exercise. Mr. Ohmart became a professor at Southeast Missouri State University in the late '60s. I wish I could have been a student of his in college, but I graduated in 1964. We enjoyed Mr. Ohmart hunting squirrels on our farm. I wish I had gone to see him while he was a professor at SEMO. It would have been fun seeing him in a university setting.

Mr. Bennie Purcell—I saved this teacher for last. The aforementioned teachers were all very good teachers who had a profound effect upon me, but Mr. Purcell was my mentor. I came to love and respect him as coach and as a person who truly cared about my welfare. He came to Anna-Jonesboro my junior year in high school and was my physical education teacher, as well as our new basketball coach. Coach Purcell was an All-American at Murray State in 1954. I didn't really get to know Coach Purcell until my senior year. I was very disappointed when I tried out for basketball my freshman year and didn't make the team. Not knowing what the future might hold for me in basketball, I had decided to try to improve.

Mr. Bennie Purcell

Determined not to give up, I worked on my own, playing ball in the old one-room Lake Hill School on our farm, and Sonny Eddleman's barn during the winter months. Larry Morgan, Sonny, and I would play for hours every Saturday. One of our favorite games was H.O.R.S.E. which improved my shooting skills tremendously. I knew the fundamentals of shooting from my junior high years, so I developed muscle memory by shooting the ball over and over and over. During my sophomore and junior years in school I continued to play basketball in physical education and on the F.F.A. team. I knew that hard work would greatly increase my chance of making the high school team. There was no guarantee that I would ever play high school basketball, but I was determined to prove I could.

I finally began to grow and reached 5'9" my junior year. I still hadn't played high school ball because of my farm duties. I was still hoping my senior year to go out for basketball. The odds would be against me since I hadn't played on the high school team the previous three years. I still had my chores; however, the transportation issue was resolved. My brother was in the Navy by then, and I would get to drive his 1953 Ford Fairlane during my senior year. At least, I would be able to get to and from basketball practice if I made the team. I was definitely enjoying my growth spurt. I had grown 8" in two years, and I was 6'1" entering my senior year in 1959. I had improved considerably in my shooting and jumping skills. I was hoping Coach Purcell would notice me. I sure worked hard to gain his approval and attention. I never did get to run track or play baseball because of farm duties, so I was really hoping to play basketball my senior year.

Bennie Purcell with his number 21 jersey that is now hanging in the Murray State University Arena. Bennie was an All-American basketball player in 1954.

Chapter 8

Values

DISCIPLINE

What do kids think of when they are disciplined? It's the nature of every child to assume the disciplinarian is just being mean. We were no different. It doesn't matter if it's coming from a teacher, the principal, or our parents. Many people say their fourth-grade year was the worst one for being disciplined. I agree. Why? The fourth-grade year is when students must really dig into math, science, reading and geography. I had a tough fourth-grade teacher, but nearly every child would say at some point that their teachers were mean. I had a fourth-grade student at Lick Creek say, "Coach Ron, you're mean!" to which I responded, "And don't you forget it!" An eighth-grade student once asked me, "Why?" My reply was, "Because I said so." When he asked me why again, he earned a "Happy Hour" (40 minutes of planks, leg raises, push-ups, isometrics, sprints, and laps.) I had been subjected to that exact discipline at the Great Lakes Naval Training Center in 1966.

Now that many years have gone by, I have more of a grasp on the meaning of discipline. I became good friends with many of my teachers later in my life. I finally understood what they wanted me to achieve. As I've gotten older, I have learned that I must discipline myself in order to achieve the things I want to accomplish. I have been working with youth for almost 50 years. It requires discipline on my part to keep students motivated to and wanting to work and to achieve. Plans have to be made; schedules have to be set. I have to focus on what I want to achieve and what I want the youth to achieve. It takes hours and hours of preparation to reach goals. The definition of self-discipline is disciplining yourself, so others won't have to.

What I didn't learn early in my career was how to get young people to understand discipline, and to heed instruction. If they associate discipline with pain, they will resist. I still have trouble with kids and discipline; however, it's not as bad as the early years. I have discovered that it's my job to find a way to make activities enjoyable. In my physical education classes, most will adhere to discipline if an event is enjoyable. Many of our drills are speed related. For example, if I ask the students to run twenty wind sprints or twenty laps, I would have more problems than if I have them running drills which require them to chase Z-balls, Frisbees, or basketballs. When they are focused on the competition, their minds forget about the work involved.

Every teacher must find a way to make their subject as exciting as possible. The level of motivation and excitement demonstrated by the teacher will determine the discipline level.

RESPECT

Recently, I received word that the fourth and fifth graders at Lick Creek were being very disrespectful during class. I also was having some problems with my physical education class talking while I was giving instruction. I said, "Kids, I'm talking, and you're talking over me. I want it stopped!"

I decided it would be a good time to teach manners and respect. I really didn't want to take time out of physical education but felt it was necessary. I started with manners. I asked what they thought manners included. Some said, "It means saying, 'Thank you,' 'Excuse me,' 'You're welcome,' 'I appreciate it,' and 'Yes, Sir,' 'Yes, Ma'am'." I saw that they knew what to do, so I asked, "Why aren't you doing it?" We talked about what it means to show respect and why manners are important. I reminded them of how disrespectful it is to interrupt people when they are talking and how rude it is to walk between people who are talking. Many times, when kids do things for me, I will say, "Thank you. I really appreciate your help." Only a few respond, "You're welcome." The reason some kids do have good manners is because their parents have taught them.

I recently spent some time with one of my former coaches at the Eldorado Holiday tournament. While I was athletic director at Jonesboro, I recommended Randy Boyd to coach basketball for the Bulldogs. Randy had suffered through a couple of seasons as he was rebuilding the program. He mentioned to me that he was getting calls from parents way into the evenings. I said, "Randy, you don't have to take calls that late, but if you do, listen to them, and be respectful. They are frustrated also." Randy's first two seasons were decent with 18 wins and 26 losses, if my memory serves me right—not horrendous, however, to a young energetic coach, patience comes slowly. I know this well. I started my career at Jonesboro going 9-13. I told Randy it takes 3-5 years to build a program. I knew that Randy was going to be a success, because I watched his practices. He was the most focused coach I'd seen in many years. If I needed to talk with him, I would wait because I never wanted to interrupt what he was saying to his players.

Randy's third year showed much improvement, and year four was the greatest season ever. They went 26-0, winning the State Championship in the 1999-2000 season. They defeated a very powerful Cairo Jr. High team, coached by Tommy Ellis, by two points. He had great respect for his players, and those players had respect for him. The two coaches

Coach Boyd celebrating his State Championship 1999.

showed so much class after the game, displaying great respect for each other. Randy commended Coach Ellis after the game. It's not very often you see that by a losing coach, especially after a two-point loss. The whole game was played with great respect and sportsmanship.

Randy recently retired as the industrial arts teacher at Carrier Mills High School. His success at Jonesboro carried over through the years.

RANDY'S STORY ABOUT RESPECT

While teaching industrial arts, Randy invited a financially successful businessman to speak to his shop class. Randy instructed the students to be attentive, to show respect, and to thank him for coming. After the speaker finished, all of the students did just that. The speaker was so impressed with the students. He was surprised that almost all of the students had firm handshakes. Parents who instill respect at an early age give their children a great start. We teachers must hammer home the value of respect to our students, just as Randy did with his class. Months later, the businessman asked Randy if he needed anything for his shop. Randy mentioned he needed some industrial arts supplies. The gentleman responded by purchasing a significant amount of supplies for the school.

Disrespect for authority is becoming more and more common, because it's not being taught in schools or at home, like it used to be. We, as parents and teachers, must make sure to instill in our kids respect for authority. We need to teach them respect for the men and women in the armed forces, police officers, firefighters, and, of course, their parents and teachers.

I believe that if every parent took the time to teach respect, boys and girls would again grow up wanting to be police officers, firefighters, and other law-enforcers. In our area, most kids show respect for law officers. However, across America, we are seeing so much violence against authority.

COMMITMENT

In my opinion one of the most powerful tools to learning is commitment. Many times, a person will make a commitment to do something, but then the novelty wears off, and the person quits. As I've said often, "Quitters never win; winners never quit." Commitment must include action. Enthusiasm energizes the commitment and gives it value. Just going through the motions is not sufficient. It's amazing what Bob Love did when he dreamed of becoming an NBA player. He overcame many obstacles. I tell him all the time how much he impressed me over the years. I believe that one knows in his or her heart if their passion is strong enough to commit. I knew that my decision to play basketball for Coach Purcell was the right decision. Commitment goes hand-in-hand with discipline. Herbert Spencer said, "The great aim of education is not knowledge but action."

Determine your goal or purpose. Then commit to it! You are not only committing to an event or a sport. You are committing to yourself.

Wealth

"To live content with small means; seek elegance rather than luxury, and refinement rather than fashion; to be worthy, not respectable, and wealthy, not rich; to study hard, think quietly, talk gently, act frankly; to listen to stars and birds, to babes and sages, with open heart; to bear all cheerfully, do all bravely; await occasions, hurry never; in a word, to let the spiritual, unbidden and unconscious grow up through the common. This is my symphony."
 – William Henry Channing 1810-1884

We all think we would love to be rich. I have observed so many wealthy people over my lifetime and have seen so much unhappiness. Hollywood is in such disarray; it makes me sad for so many of those people who are searching for happiness. God has given them so much talent. I can name many who have committed suicide over the years, and I ask, "What did they lack?" The problem can be summed up in one word, "materialism." It is the drive to always want more, to accumulate material things to gain social status, money, or both. It means "more" is never enough. Soon a void sets in. People wake up and say, "I'm not satisfied. Why am I not happy?" Possessions can only provide temporary happiness. Many comedians who have died over the past few years could make people laugh, yet they themselves were unhappy. Self-worth and net worth are not the same. God tells us the most valuable things are not things. I also have witnessed the rat race of people trying to chase financial gain while at the same time totally stressing themselves out.

I spent 16 years as a Regional Manager for Rogers Benefit Group, a marketing firm for Principal Mutual Life out of Des Moines, Iowa. I was a health insurance representative for four states. I was successful and met many people, and established relationships that I cherish to this day. But as much as I enjoyed my 16 years with the marketing firm, my most enjoyable times were my evenings coaching Anna Jr. High School 5th and 6th graders and coaching the Saturday morning programs at Jonesboro. It's obvious which job paid the better salary! My greatest satisfaction was watching those young athletes develop into good athletes and good citizens. Self-worth is more important than net worth. Success is not found in things!

THE IMPORTANCE OF SELF-ESTEEM

This is something that I struggled with growing up. It's true. One reason was my small stature. Self-esteem is how you feel about yourself. I was, for some reason, shy and insecure. I was always so afraid I was going to be called on in class. I would slump down so the teacher wouldn't see me. Bob Love told me he did the same thing. His reason was a disability called stuttering. I was a fairly good student. I could spell, write, and do math well. The low self-esteem continued into my high school years. In FFA, I was on the debate team and rarely opened my mouth. We all live in an area that we feel good about—it's called "a comfort zone." My fear of saying the wrong

130

thing was most of the problem. That fear could literally shut me down or prevent me from even starting something. Franklin Delano Roosevelt said, "The only thing we have to fear is fear itself." Relief came in my freshman year at Southeast Missouri State University in 1960. I was required to take speech, which meant I had to give a speech in front of other students. I didn't have a choice. I either had to do it or fail my freshman year at the outset. I was afraid, but I had to just do it! My speech was on how the self-propelled combine works. Many of the students were from the Saint Louis area, and they didn't have a clue about how a piece of farm equipment worked. I chose a topic that made me as comfortable as possible. From that day forward I gained confidence in speaking.

In my careers as teacher, coach, insurance representative, national safety associate representative, and health and safety director, I have spoken to thousands of people over the past 50 years. I thank God that I made that speech at SEMO that day in 1960.

ESTABLISHING GOALS WITH PURPOSE

I'm a goal-setting person. Since much of my life has been in coaching, marketing, and sales, I have been goal-oriented. Before a person takes action, he must first know what he wants. Goals have played a major role in:

- Planning basketball practices
- Conducting speed camps

- Planning lessons for physical education classes
- Setting standards for my insurance agents
- Setting goals for health fairs and fitness seminars

Goals must have meaning, otherwise what is the purpose? If you're going to drive west to Seattle, Washington, like I did in 1966, you first must have a plan and a goal. I needed a road map. My purpose was that I had to check in at the Puget Sound Naval Torpedo Station on a certain date. My plan had to be thought out on how long the trip was going to take, and how I was going to get there. What routes would I have to take in order to get me to the Naval Base at the appointed time?

In coaching or in my speed camps, I needed drills that would improve the athletes' performances. The purpose was to use the drills that would be most effective for the many different fundamentals required for the sport that I was teaching. Goals also help keep a person on schedule. Goal-setting and planning are important for being organized. Disorganization is inefficient. Without organization, the wheels come off the bus. The habit of being late all the time is a consequence of not being organized. Setting planning goals greatly helps overcome this bad habit. I always had a black date book for keeping track of important meetings and functions. The date, time, and location were entered so I could focus on the main issues. Budget your time. It is a valuable commodity; don't waste it. I tell my physical education classes if they are goofing around, "Hey, troops! We are burning time!" We have to take charge of our time, or the time will take over, and we will fail in our purpose.

Chapter 9
My Philosophy

WHAT IS LIFE ALL ABOUT?

Some people never seem to know what God wants for their life. We are all focused on something. That something should have meaning. Thomas Carlyle wrote, "The man without a purpose is like a ship without a rudder—a waif, a nothing, a no man." Today the average life span is 25,550 days. I'm already over that number by 3,000 days. We have to figure out what is important as we live out our lives.

I have devoted much of my life to working with youth, both at the public schools and the church. My mother made sure my brother and I were always in Sunday school and church. We had a good start through the spiritual training we received from Mother and the church. One must have a firm foundation to be successful in life. "A life devoted to THINGS is a dead life, a stump; a God-shaped life is a flourishing tree." Proverbs 11:28 (The Message). Focusing on ourselves will never reveal our life's purpose. Lives driven by greed, selfishness, and materialism will bring heartache. It's not about us. It's about others. We need others in our lives. I am so happy I get to be a part of the Lick Creek School and Lick Creek community. Many schools and communities are dysfunctional. Living in Jonesboro and working at the Jonesboro Grade School for 17 years was also a fruitful time. When schools, churches, and communities work together, wonderful things happen. What I've observed while working in the Lick Creek School District is the community's outpouring of love and concern for the school. What is even more amazing is the financial support demonstrated when we have our PTO Fall Festival and the Tom Sherrill Memorial Golf Scramble. Thousands and thousands of dollars have been raised by many people all over Union County.

Money has even come in from Washington, D.C., and many southern Illinois towns and surrounding counties. It's simply amazing to see that level of love and concern for our educational endeavors. My goal has been, "Who can I help today?" Working with youth is so rewarding. We can't put a monetary amount on it. The satisfaction of seeing a child learn a new drill in physical education is so beautiful. Their faces light up like Christmas trees. When I observe this, my face lights up also!

Back to the subject of goals. A person needs to figure out what he or she is good at. Believe you can achieve whatever you set out to do. Involve others. By involving others, you will enjoy reaching the goal even more. Make sure you don't try to do too much. Try to keep stress out of your life as much as possible. Keep past bad memories of your life out of the present. Past set-backs can't be changed. We must let go of resentment and bitterness over past events or personal encounters. I've had parents resent me. When that happens, I try to make amends, however it doesn't always happen. No one can make a person change their mind if they choose not to. I admit that I've made mistakes, and some of the resentment toward me is deserved. But our job is to let go of the resentment we feel towards others.

We all like to have approval. We all want everyone to like us. That is never going to happen. There is constant pressure from teachers, coaches, parents, and others to conform in a certain way. We must be able to handle this daily pressure. If you try to please everyone, you will fail miserably. I remember working with Dad, and he would tell me how he wanted something done on the farm. I resisted many times because I thought I had a better way of doing it. I would get so mad I could bite nails in two. Ninety-five percent of the time Dad knew much more than I did because of his experience. The Bible says, "Do not provoke your child to anger." I think I provoked myself to anger! If cell phones had existed back in the '50s, and Dad had taken a picture of my angry face, my students at Lick Creek would get a kick out of it. One thing I did do was let my displeasure be known. We have to be careful not to bottle up our displeasures and anger. Some people hang on to their anger for many years. I hung on to many of those mad moments, but only to laugh about them with Dad as we remembered the times we shared as a father/son team. If we have hurt that we have developed resentment over, and we develop bitterness and hate, we are only hurting ourselves. The Bible says,

"To worry yourself to death with resentment would be a foolish, senseless thing to do."

I'm so thankful that I had the opportunity to work alongside Mom and Dad during my growing-up years. Those memories have never faded. I wish more youth today could have the same opportunity that I had. I know some have. Rick Uvesay is one who comes to mind. I did some work for Rick's dad on the Ware farm. I watched Rick working with his dad, doing some of the same things that I did with my dad.

Handling Wealth

It's a sad thing to see successful people who have earned many awards during their careers and have thrown them away. Why? They were driven by greed. Material things became the goal. I have seen so many great athletes who have earned millions of dollars and have thrown it away. They chose the wrong purpose and goals for their lives. They always want more stuff. I have seen athletes signing 50 and 100 million-dollar contracts, then later, when the next contract rolls around, they are negotiating for more money. It's very difficult to earn that kind of money and stay normal. A few seem able to do it, but many can't. It's a tragedy. Some might say, "If I had that kind of money, it certainly wouldn't be a tragedy." But think about it. So many obstacles get in the way of wisdom—lavish living, mismanagement, and poor financial decisions. Many have been duped by unscrupulous people.

It is encouraging that many successful billionaires like Bill Gates have kept their purpose for living in proper perspective. They have the foresight to give millions of dollars to charities and other organizations. They purpose to help people by giving back.

IT'S NOT MY FAULT

I have worked with youth for many years, and I hear this statement almost every day, "It's not my fault!" Kids are notorious for saying it. I hear things like, "John made me do it," and "I was just standing there, and Jeff hit me." Nearly every day, when the students line up after a class period is over, I hear something like, "Luke 'cutted' me in line." They will shove and push to get in front of someone. I always say, "Why are you in such a hurry to get back to class?" What usually happens is the "pushers" get a few laps and are the last ones back to class. I'm sure I did the same thing when I was their age, especially in kindergarten through second grade.

Human nature in children is so fascinating. After years of observation, I am usually able to identify the source of a problem. When something happens, I can usually trace it back to the one making the accusation. Many times, the incident was created by the accuser. Primary school kids love to tattle, and most kids have trouble taking responsibility for their own actions. That's where we as teachers and parents can help them to grow and mature into well- rounded adults.

Sometimes, we as adults still have problems with responsibility and accountability. Have you ever said something like this, "Honey, I put my keys on the table. What did you do with them?" The wife says, "I never saw your keys. Why are you blaming me?" And you say, "Well, they didn't just jump off the table!" The most common outcome is that the keys turn up somewhere else, and the accuser has to admit sheepishly, "I thought I left the keys on the table, but I found them on top of the dresser." Human nature in adults is fascinating. FYI, I never did anything like this. Ask Paula.

HEALTH AND HAPPINESS

I have been so blessed with good health over my lifetime. Health is more than just not being sick. Health is how you feel about life, how you go about your day, your outlook. It's your aliveness, your joy. I believe your health is direct related to how you interact with people. It's all about relationships. It's about being positive and seeing people in a loving, kind way. It's doing things you enjoy. It might be a hobby or the job you love. Millions of people go to work each day who hate what they are doing. If you're in a job you don't like, fatigue will set in. Your immune system can be affected by how you feel about things. When I ask some people how they are doing, I get a litany of physical reasons about why they can't get things done. My advice is to use your body—get up and get going. It's your body; use it or lose it. Americans have a more sedentary life style now, more than ever before. We have so many electronic devices that didn't exist in the '40s and '50s. Obesity is rampant, and being overweight makes it harder to move. It's a vicious cycle. Find your passion, and go after it. It is contagious. "Life is a great adventure or nothing at all." (Helen Keller) I know my great adventure is working with youth. I hope you find yours.

Rich Herrin is a good friend whom I have admired for more than 40 years. We have worked together in coaching clinics and have always enjoyed talking basketball. Rich never lost his love for coaching and life. The Benton Gymnasium is named in Rich's honor. He was an outstanding coach at Benton High School where he won many South Seven Conference titles.

He needs no introduction for his success at Southern Illinois University at Carbondale, where he won several Missouri Valley Conference titles. He has been inducted into the Illinois Basketball Coaches Association Hall of Fame, the Missouri Valley Hall of Fame, and Southern Illinois University's Hall of Fame. He found what he loved, and he pursued it. He never asked himself if he was good enough; he only asked himself if he loved to do it. He is a great Christian man and a wonderful mentor. He's still on fire with his passion. He joined me and the golfers at the 8th Annual Tom Sherrill Memorial Golf Scramble this past September. Rich has always been very healthy, but now that he is in his late 80s, he has some physical ailments. But that hasn't kept him away from the gymnasium. I've seen Rich talking to fans at Goreville, SIU, and Eldorado, continuing to enjoy his passion.

I was visiting with Chris Wells at the Anna-Jonesboro National Bank recently, and we were discussing our fitness schedules. I mentioned that I still arrive at Lick Creek School every morning at 6:00 a.m. to work out. Chris, who now lives in Paducah, Kentucky, still maintains a rigorous fitness schedule. I asked him, "Chris, with all the education we now have on health, diet, and fitness, why do we see so many people in poor health?" We discussed the reasons and came to the conclusion that people do know about good health practices. However, the desire for unhealthy foods so readily available is like the craving for a cigarette. The food tastes so good to them they just can't help themselves. It's instant gratification. "Junk" food wasn't available 50 years ago. Fast-food restaurants are ubiquitous in most cities. We, as a society, don't want to think about what these foods are doing to our bodies. Fast food is okay if eaten in moderation, however, promotional offers on supersized foods seems to override people's thinking processes. Widespread obesity means many ailments are now showing up in early adulthood. Diabetes and joint problems caused by excessive weight are creating a crisis in America. Sedentary lives prevent people from burning the number of calories that fueled people's active lifestyles 40 years ago.

I realize some people have hereditary issues when it comes to health. Most of us experienced childhood diseases. My point is that many illnesses can be prevented by proper diet, exercise, and mental attitude.

THE WINNER CREED

I have a set of principles I have established based on my own observations about life and what it takes to be a winner. I've condensed many things about life into this creed. Much of my assessment on life and athletics has been attained from many of my mentors and coaches over the years. I don't claim to have all the answers. The ideas I have gathered from these people, along with my experience working with youth, has helped me formulate what I think it takes to excel in both athletics and life itself. In order to succeed, accountability and responsibility are always necessary to remove any doubt or obstacles one may encounter. When I hear excuses about why success was not achieved, I recognize the poison. Excuses are killers! An excuse is not taking responsibility, and it's easy for it to become a habit. That removes accountability of one's actions in their own mind. Making excuses is rampant in our society.

We must set a higher standard. While coaching at Jonesboro, Anna Jr. High, New Simpson Hill, and Anna-Jonesboro, I always set a goal to win a certain number of games and to improve on fundamentals.

In the classroom, I ask the students to set goals and work hard. Students and athletes who achieve the best are those who are motivated. We must develop a clear plan of action. Being satisfied with mediocrity will never allow any kind of success. If a leader, a coach, or a teacher accepts mediocrity, it will affect the whole team or class. Try to push out any negatives that might be present. If negative attitudes are creeping into the class, unit, individual, or team, they must be dealt with immediately.

The importance of good decision-making is essential. If a coach or teacher isn't having success, it may be that the right decisions aren't being made. In the case of a coach who isn't having success, he or she might need to think of ways to improve performance. In my experience as coach, teacher, and athletic director, I've seen so many coaches who have excelled. However, in the programs that have had little success, I believe the main culprit is an unwillingness to change. A teacher or coach who isn't willing to adapt the curriculum or the sport is doomed to mediocrity or even failure. Doing the same things over and over without success will lead to frustration. Successful leaders don't make excuses all the time or play the blame game. What they do is adapt, prepare, and study the situation, and then make the appropriate adjustments. Successful teachers and coaches also attend seminars and clinics and seek individual improvement. Good decision-making, self-discipline, effective training, and sound beliefs are foundational for every teacher or coach.

1. Coaches must teach players to believe in themselves. Believing is achieving. Schools with rich traditions have developed this important essential. They see to it that their team is physically fit with high intensity practices. The practice schedule is set up so there isn't any down time. Efficiency is so important. Practices that waste time are not efficient. Standing around or sitting in the bleachers is not going to produce success.

2. Teachers must be able to discipline. Without discipline there is very little learning. They must be able to motivate students to want to learn and achieve. If the teacher isn't excited, there won't be much excitement from the students. Teachers should be well-prepared, and like coaches, utilize their time wisely.

3. For students, self-discipline and good study habits are imperative.

QUOTES ABOUT WINNING

Ability is what you're capable of doing.
Motivation determines what you do.
Attitude determines how well you do it.
— Lou Holtz

Winners concentrate on winning; losers
concentrate on getting by.
— John Maxwell

Before a person can achieve the kind of
life he wants, he must think, act, walk, talk,
and conduct himself in all of his affairs as
would the person he wishes to become.
— Zig Ziglar

If you have a will to win, you have
achieved half of your success; if you
don't, you have achieved half your failure.
— David Ambrose

Always do more than is required of you.
— General George S. Patton

Man creates his environment—mental,
emotional, and physical—by the attitude
he develops.
— Author Unknown

Prioritize and execute. Do what is most important. Spending time on trivial matters is wasted time, when more important issues need to be addressed. Sometimes we will put off the hardest things and do the easiest first. That is where we make the mistake.
– Jocko Willink and Leif Babin, Navy Seals, in
Extreme Ownership

Chapter 10

People I Appreciate

I have shared my message with many people over the years and, while doing so, they have shared their lives with me. I'm so grateful to have known and worked with these people.

EDWARD M. SMITH

I knew Ed as a high school basketball player at Shawnee High School in the 1960s. I didn't know him personally at first, only that he was a fine basketball player. It wasn't until the mid-'90s that I got to know Ed. His son Matt was a student at Jonesboro Grade School where I was Athletic Director. I had a Saturday morning basketball program that I started in 1970. I ran the program each Saturday morning during the months of November through March. (My granddaughter Amanda was in the same fourth grade class as Matt. Amanda was living with us while her mom and dad finished the year as correctional guards at Statesville Prison in Joliet, Illinois. They were going to be transferred to the Vienna Correctional facility, so we decided to have Amanda stay with us while the transition took place.)

I met Ed the first Saturday of our basketball program. After a few Saturdays, we talked about playing some 3-on-3 or 4-on-4 games after the morning session ended. Bill Littrell, another great friend, and his daughter Stella and son Perry wanted to participate. The first Saturday we gathered to play, I saw that Ed was wearing a pair of P.N. Hirsch tennis shoes. I asked, "How long has it been since you played—fifteen years?!" That was the beginning of a long friendship.

I retired from my insurance business in 1994 and was available to start another career. I continued to work with youth. I'm in my 50th year working with youth and still love it very much. I had been doing some work in a marketing business for about three years and was ready to get into another challenging career.

Ed & Betty Smith knew I had retired and asked if I might be interested in being a health insurance benefit representative for the Laborers' Union. I accepted the challenge and began my new career in July of 1997, working for the Southern Illinois Health & Welfare Fund located in Cairo, Illinois. I was back in the insurance business. I was promoted a few years later to the Midwest Health and Safety Director for the seven Midwest States. I retired again and started another career —my second as a teacher—at Lick Creek School District #16 in Buncombe, Illinois. I worked seven years with the Laborers' Union. Because my office was in Springfield, Illinois, traveling back and forth to my job was taxing, so I returned to Southern Illinois as a retiree benefit representative until 2004. In 2006, I was employed by the Lick Creek school board. I'm in my 13th

146

year as a physical education teacher. I have been privileged to have worked with many children over this time. I have met so many parents and grandparents. Little did I know, back in 1969, while teaching and coaching at Jonesboro, I would end my career at Lick Creek. One thing that is great about this job is that about 15 of my Jonesboro eighth graders from the early '70s have grandchildren that are in my classes now. It's kind of fun waiting on grandparents at Grandparents Day who used to be my eighth-grade students.

Ed & Betty Smith offered me a great new challenge. He became my boss and also a great friend. Ed has been a faithful supporter of the Lick Creek School Educational Foundation over the past ten years. He and Betty were also instrumental in helping establish the Therapy Center in Carterville. They also have been active in their support of the Shawnee Community College in Ullin, Illinois.

CAPT. ROBERT W. DUNCAN, UNITED STATES NAVY ACE WWII

My son-in-law Doug Killebrew owned Aeroflite, Inc. and invited Paula and I to the Williamson County Air show in Marion, Illinois. Upon arriving I immediately spotted Capt. Duncan sitting in the front row at the airport runway with a couple of empty seats beside him. We walked up and introduced ourselves to the veteran pilot. I told him that I'd served in the Navy in the 1960s. He was in full uniform with the "scrambled eggs" embroidered on the bill of his cap. I was so honored to meet him.

Captain Robert W. Duncan

He invited us to sit with him and watch the air show. I wanted to learn as much as I could about him and his career as a naval officer. The WWII Ace Pilot, a naval war hero, was even in the Naval Hall of Fame. We watched the show together and then set a date to meet at the Cracker Barrel in Marion. Capt. Duncan was 84-years-old when we met in 2004. Our meetings at the Cracker Barrel became more frequent, as we became more acquainted with each another. It was fascinating to hear him talk firsthand about the many missions that he flew. I was substitute teaching at the time at the Vienna, New Simpson Hill, and Cypress schools and invited Capt. Duncan to speak to the students at both the Vienna and New Simpson Hill grade schools. Four years later, I was teaching full-time at Lick Creek School District #16, so my World Events class invited him to come and share his WWII experience. The students from all those schools still talk about how awesome those meetings were. I never tired of hearing his stories. Upon Captain Duncan's arrival at the Lick Creek School, I had all the students line up on the entrance sidewalk. Each student held a small flag, and each saluted him as he entered the school. I had goose bumps and a lump in my throat. Capt. Duncan, now in his late eighties, was limited in his ability to communicate, but we still enjoyed listening to him speak in very soft tones. We were even able to pull up an interview he had done a few years earlier on the History Channel. It was so cool to sit right next to him while we listened to him talk about his war experience on TV. I will never forget it, nor will the students. Fleet Admiral Chester Nimitz, the U.S. Supreme Allied Commander in the South Pacific, was his boss while he was stationed in San Francisco.

Capt. Duncan's missions were mainly in the South Pacific. He was credited with seven Japanese kills in the air and six more on the ground. He found out years later one of his victims was the top Ace pilot of the Japanese who had nine kills. He flew off the famed aircraft carrier USS *Yorktown* (The Fighting Lady). He was the first pilot to have flown off the carrier to bring down a Japanese Zero. After WWII, he served in the Korean War and worked in the office of the Chief of Naval Operations in the Pentagon.

BEN DUNN – WWII HERO

I first got to know Ben Dunn while he was the superintendent in the early '70s at the Anna-Jonesboro Community High School. He was guest speaker at one of my sports banquets, and in more recent years, had been a guest celebrity at the Tom Sherrill Memorial Golf Classic for the Lick Creek School's Educational Foundation.

Ben Dunn was always passionate about education. His early teaching career was interrupted by WWII. Ben served in Southeast Asia as a member of the field artillery and was captured in March of 1942. For three years he remained a prisoner of war working on the infamous Death Railway, and then was sent to the Japanese prison camp at River Kwai (Burma-Thailand). Refusing to give up, Ben miraculously survived unimaginable hardships before being liberated in August of 1945. That POW camp inspired screen writers to produce the movie "Bridge on The River Kwai" starring William Holden and Alex Guinness. It was a very accurate depiction of the very camp Ben was in.

Ben returned to teach history and coach at Gorham, Illinois. He was one of the greatest baseball coaches of all time. During his career he coached over 40 college, minor, and major league baseball teams. His most notable players were Joe Grace and Gary Geiger. Gary played alongside one of the greatest players ever, the great Ted Williams of the Boston Red Sox. Ted was the last player to bat over .400 (in 1941 when he batted .406.)

Private Dunn and Captain Duncan both kept the students spellbound as they told their stories. It was an honor I will never forget. Not one but two WWII heroes came to our school while the students waved American

Fen Dunn Talking to my world events class

flags and saluted them. I'm so glad our young students could hear their stories. Their experiences defined who they were. Not many WWII veterans are still with us. Both Capt. Duncan and Ben Dunn are deceased, but never forgotten.

Bob Love, Chicago Bulls Four-Time NBA All-Star

I felt strongly about telling the story of Bob Love's life because it addresses what it takes to overcome adversity and to strive to be a success. In my opinion, nothing compares to the adversity that Bob encountered throughout his life. When Bob appeared with Capt. Robert W. Duncan and Benjamin Dunn at the Tom Sherrill Memorial Golf Scramble, he said, "I was an All-American at Southern University in Baton Rouge, Louisiana. These men were All-American heroes during WWII." Bob said they had encountered a different kind of adversity than he had. "Theirs was life threatening! They are the true All-Americans." Bob seemed really pleased to share the platform with them.

I was privileged to work and socialize with my friend Bob for more than 17 years. I first worked with him when I was the Health & Safety Director for the Laborers' International Union of North America. Bob was asked to be the motivational speaker at many of the union meetings and health fairs. Also, many of the Union and Johnson County youth have attended the Bob Love Sport Speed Development and Basketball 101 camps over the past 26 years at the Vienna Grade School, Lick Creek, and Jonesboro Grade Schools, Vienna High School, Anna-Jonesboro High School, and the New Simpson Hill School.

Many older people remember Bob playing for the Chicago Bulls in the late '60s and '70s. Bob held most of the Bulls' records until a fellow named Michael Jordan broke nearly all of them in his playing career during the '80s and '90s.

Few people know what Bob Love had to overcome to make it in life. Today, many people play the role of a victim. Bob refused to be the "victim" of anything. Growing up on a plantation in Delhi, Louisiana, he was raised in a two-room house with 13 siblings. He was abused by a stepfather and forced to go live with his grandmother at a very young age. But he overcame adversity and became a great role model.

Maxine E. Fulenwider

My mother's influence on my life was tremendous. This tribute to my mother was given at the First Christian Church, Anna, Illinois, 1987, at the mother-daughter Mother's Day Banquet.

So many favorite memories of my mom have stayed with me over the years, and many of them contain valuable lessons on life.

I would imagine there is no spectacle on earth more pleasing to God than my mom preparing a meal for her family. Bruce and Dad will tell you the same thing. Often, she would sing a beautiful hymn as she was preparing the meal. Her face seemed almost lit up. My wife Paula's face lights up when she is cooking also. She reminds me of my mom, especially when she is cooking.

Mom's enduring love, patience, and understanding were so special. Bruce and I had so much security. We were made to feel special because of our parents' love for us. We remember Mom humming or singing hymns like "It is No Secret What God Can Do" and "Jesus Loves the Little Children." That was so special. Our relationship with Mom was so sweet. We know we were fortunate to have her.

When we came in from school, we'd holler, "Hey, Mom! I'm home!" I can't remember a day she wasn't home when I arrived from school. She would have a sandwich or cereal ready for me. Often, the "Howdy Doody" show would be on, and we would watch the show together. I felt so loved. The mothers at Lick Creek Preschool (Class of 2014) always wondered why I would come in each noon hour with their lunch and ask, "What time is it, boys and girls?" The children would say, "It's Howdy Doody Time, Coach Ron." Once, they even got to see a Howdy Doody film from the early 1950s, and they loved it as much as I did when I watched it with my mother.

Mom is second from the right with her many friends.

Mom also was our spiritual guide. She always made sure we were dressed for Sunday school. She read the Bible to us, prayed with us, taught us to pray, and taught us Bible songs. On the way to Sunday school I can still hear her say, "You didn't wash your face." That meant we would get a spit-washing job done on us when we arrived at the First Baptist Church in Jonesboro.

Henry Ward Beecher said, "A mother's heart is the child's schoolroom." Everything you need to know is right there for the asking. Mother is all the ingredients of your life wrapped into one spiritual package.

Mom handled the chores, took care of us when sickness came, and soothed our boo-boos. She could make minor burns, smashed fingers, scratches, or cuts feel better with a simple kiss. It was tremendously therapeutic! I love it now when my little kindergarten kids come up to me with a little scratch and ask for a band-aid. They just need sympathy. I usually say, "It does look pretty bad," and get them a band-aid. It brings back precious memories of my mom caring for Bruce and me the same way.

The most important fundamental institution of society is the home. Children spend the most hours in the home, especially in their first five or six years. It's the major factor in their social development. It is even more important in our society today because of uncensored TV, movies (the rating system is a farce), alcohol, drugs, sex, and greater peer pressure.

Kate Douglas Wiggin said, "There is only one mother. Most all other beautiful things come in two or three, or by dozens or hundreds. There are plenty of roses, stars, sunsets, rainbows, brothers, sisters, cousins, and aunts—but only one mother in the whole world."

Paula K. Fulenwider

The two biggest influences in my life have been my mom and my wife, Paula. God certainly gave me another chance in life when I met Paula in the winter of 1983. She was employed by the Honorable Paul Simon, United States Congressman. Paul once told me how much he thought of Paula, and what a great employee she was. That sure carried a lot of weight with me. I had the privilege of driving Paul around Southern Illinois a few times when he was running for Congressman. He was such an enjoyable person to be around. The Paul Simon Political Institution in Carbondale, Illinois is named for him. Paul passed away several years ago. It was a tremendous loss for Southern Illinois when he passed away.

I was introduced to Paula Ashman by Sandy Herring, my administrative assistant. Sandy, who lived in Murphysboro, Illinois, told me that Paula was single. I made a phone call, and we began dating. From that point on, our relationship grew. My mom and dad were instantly in

I am dining with Paula at a Laborers' function. To our right is Betty Smith, Health & Welfare Administrator.

love with Paula, and Paula likewise with them. She learned their personalities quickly, especially regarding my dad, who could be somewhat of an instigator. (I'm sure glad I didn't follow in my dad's footsteps in that category!) The day I met Paula, one of her daughters (Julie) was at her home. She was holding a beautiful little three-month-old baby named Amanda.

That little one had a lot to do with my initial interest in Paula. It was the beginning of a new chapter in my life. Like myself, Paula had two daughters, Julie and Amy. They were both very close in age to my own two daughters.

After nine months, Paula and I were married and have been for 35 years. Our girls all get along great. I rarely call Paula's two daughters my step-daughters. I just say, "These are my daughters, Julie and Amy." Paula does the same with my daughters, Leigh and Loretta. Paula gets the sweetest cards from both of my girls, and it's such a blessing. Sadly, that kind of love and respect isn't common in many homes today. Our girls all get together when they can. A few years ago, Loretta and her husband Doug lived in Fort Mill, South Carolina, close to where Amy and her husband were living. (I have three sons-in-law named Doug.) The year that Doug and Loretta lived in Fort Mill, they were able to get together with Doug and Amy, and the two couples grew close. It seemed God had a hand in developing that relationship. All four daughters are in their early 50s now, and Paula and I are so glad they all get along so well.

Paula understands me more and knows me better than anyone else. She has been married to two coaches over 54 years, which is to say she is an amazing lady! She was married to Tom for 19 years and to me for 35. She stuck with me, and we made it work. Was it easy? Not always, but Paula sacrificed and supported me through the tough years. I no longer bench coach, but I'm very much involved with my Lick Creek students. After 50 years of teaching, coaching, selling insurance, and managing health benefits, I now work only in the mornings at Lick Creek. It wasn't always easy, and sometimes I said the wrong thing. At other times I would be out of sorts and not very good company. I've always been competitive, so, after a loss, I could be very difficult. Paula still supported me and stuck with me. She is my best friend, and I couldn't have made it without her. I know I haven't said "Thank you" enough. At one point I worked with youth and sold insurance at the same time. Then I was bench coaching and selling insurance at the same time. Those are two highly competitive situations. Paula handled it well. Coaching didn't pay very well, but because my coaching and insurance careers were successful, we did very well financially.

Paula cared about me, where I was going, and what I was doing. She always supported me and cared for me. She invested extra effort to keep our relationship strong, and she's a superb cook and homemaker. After a few tough years, we finally began to complement each other.

After retiring from the insurance business, we worked together in sales doing educational, environmental, and food supplements. We did that for four years, and together, we made it to qualifying national marketing directors with National Safety Associates out of Memphis, Tennessee. It was a great four years working together. We retired from that business because it required a lot of time and travel. Since we were financially secure, we decided on a different direction.

158

Both Paula and I have been so blessed over the years. All of the careers we have had have been wonderful. We both love people, and people are what make careers satisfying.

A Poem for My Sweet Wife, Paula

"You Will Always Be My Best Friend"
By Barbara Lantosca

Some time ago
I received a special gift,
And it came in the form of you,
My best friend.

You are so important to me,
And I want to thank you
for all the wonderful memories.

Whenever I see you,
I am reminded of myself.
Whenever I think of you,
I am reminded of the
good times we've had.

Together we've done so much,
Seen so much and felt so much.

With a knowing smile,
I look back at the shared times
and all the things only you and I know.
With high hopes and great expectations,
I look ahead to the future
and all the things only you and I will share.

You not only put a smile on my face;
You put a smile in my heart.
You will always be my best friend.

OTHERS WHO WERE IMPORTANT TO ME

I have been privileged to have coached or been associated with so many great people. Many of them made a lasting impact on my life. I wish I could see all of them again. Many have moved away or passed away. I am blessed to still see many of them, and we talk about the good times we have shared many years ago.

My first book highlighted many of the people referenced above. I wish I could list all of the youth, church, and business people with whom I have been associated. Since I have spent over 50 years working with youth, just the list of kids would be extremely long.

Coach Bernie Purcell

I have mentioned Coach Purcell earlier, but he had such a tremendous influence in my life, I'd like to finish out this chapter with him. He shaped my life in so many ways. He believed in me, and he instilled discipline and respect for authority in me. He made me understand that you can't just sit back and dream, you have to sacrifice and work hard. The hard work I'd learned on the farm came to fruition on his basketball court, but it was Coach Purcell's influence that propelled me successfully through life.

Chapter 11

Final Thoughts

As I mentioned in the introduction of this book, growing up in southern Illinois and Little Egypt during the '40s, '50s, and '60s prepared me for life's many challenges over the past 60 years. The years on the farm taught me responsibility, work ethic, and discipline. I thank my mom and dad, and my second grandparents, the Meisenheimers, for the motivation and encouragement they gave me. The work habits developed on our farm, and the neighbor's farm were very valuable. I wish young people today could have the same opportunities that I had. Modern farming doesn't utilize manual labor like it used to. Seventy pound hay bales are rarely seen today. Most bales now weigh over a thousand pounds and are picked up by a prong mounted on a tractor. Labor costs require farmers to farm differently today. Also, modernization of equipment has eliminated the need for much manual labor. The little 8N Ford tractor that I used looks like a toy tractor compared to today's big models.

THE GREAT LAKES TRAINING CENTER

The military taught rules, and one must follow them! Many incoming recruits never got that message. By week twelve, however, 95 percent of them did. I was drafted into the U.S. Army in 1965, one year out of college. It didn't matter that I was married. In December of 1965, I reported to St. Louis for my military physical. I was given the option of what branch of the service I would like. My brother Bruce was in the Navy, so that's what I chose. I never regretted selecting the Navy. The Vietnam War was beginning, and the draft had been reinstated.

I reported to the Great Lakes Training Center on April 22, 1966. We were taken by bus to St. Louis' Union Station. We arrived late in the evening and were met by some of the nicest, sweetest men I have ever met! Of course, I'm being facetious. The company commanders were waiting for us and immediately herded us off to our quarters. We are all very tired, and the unkind treatment was quite unnerving. I observed quite a bit of stress on the faces of some of the teenagers. Most of those kids were only 17 or 18 years old. We were told to go to bed, and morning wakeup would be at 5:00 a.m. None of us knew anything or anybody, so it was a pretty rude awakening. Of course, the company commanders wanted it that way. They were watching the new recruits for one reason, and that was to see our reaction to all of the hoopla! Many of those guys had never been away from home. Some were even crying, and that didn't set well with the commanders. All it did was show them which what buttons to push. We'd hear, "We have some cry-babies with us. Bless their little hearts." Expletives were the norm. I'd never heard people called so many different names.

I began to value the hard work I'd been accustomed to on the farm. Day one started with each of us being crowded into the bathroom (called heads) to brush our teeth and shower. The military's job was to mold us into a unit of sailors, and that required discipline. Then we reported to the military clothing store where we turned in our civilian clothing and were issued uniforms. After receiving our clothing, we had to label everything with our name and service number. Next came the barber shop. That was hilarious! Some had hair as long as most women. The transformation was amazing. One could tell it was not much fun for some of them. I already had a crew cut, so my transformation was minor. All military personnel wore very short hair, but Coach Purcell had also required it for his teams, so it wasn't a big deal for me. I did feel sorry for some of the recruits. They were very young, and many were obviously pampered. I would help them when I could with inspection, and other things like making up their bed tightly.

NAVAL CLASSIFICATION TESTS

The next procedure was to classify each of us (The General Classification Test Battery). That would help the Navy to select an appropriate career pattern for each person. I was immediately classified as the division's Athletic Petty Officer. My records had already disclosed my experience with college athletics. Success within the Navy is measured in terms of advancement. Those who refused to understand that concept were discharged before ever finishing training. The Navy wants men with a work ethic, discipline, and a willingness to be part of a team. It's where I learned the saying, "One for all, and all for one."

My physical education classes understand what that means. If one student messes up, the whole group has messed up. It seems cruel, but I got really familiar with it while in training. A recruit not marching properly or another doing an about face the wrong way would call for a "Happy Hour." Whenever we marched, the young man in front of me would inevitably turn the wrong way. We had rifles on our shoulders, and I was always ducking to keep from getting hit in the head. One guy in my company contacted his U.S. Congressman. That was a no-no! Of course, a congressman wouldn't pay attention to a call like that. The individual just brought more problems on himself.

Most of those individuals grew up without learning discipline or a work ethic. Many young people today would have major problems if the draft were ever brought back.

The Navy standard taught us responsibility (no blame game allowed), conduct, and manners. "Sir, yes, Sir!!!" "Ok" or "yeah" were totally unacceptable. We learned the importance of teamwork in joint tasks and responsibility of the individual towards one another. That definitely helped me in my first coaching job at Jonesboro Grade School. We learned to march in unison. We marched to breakfast, lunch, and dinner. We marched to church and to the movies. We marched in the pavilion in front of our company commander. We marched everywhere. Last but not least, we marched at graduation in front of our parents, family, and hundreds of other people.

RELIGIOUS LIFE IN THE NAVY

When we entered the military, we were given the opportunity to attend the church of our choice. I was pleased to have the opportunity to go to church, and my mother was very happy that we had church services. We had a large turn-out among my company. I would say 75% or so attended. We also had access to a chaplain at all times. The young man who called his congressmen should have called the chaplain instead. He might have made it through boot camp. Many of the young men were away from home for the first time, so having church and a spiritual guide was very important.

RECREATION CENTER

Although recruit training was regimented, and the schedule was already planned, the Navy did recognize the necessity of providing recreation to satisfy the varying interests and energies of individuals. The training center had a bowling alley, T.V. lounges, swimming pools, gymnasiums, libraries, and recreation centers for card games, shuffleboard, pool, and ping pong.

GRADUATION DAY

We finally made it to graduation after nine weeks of training. My mom and dad came, along with my wife and her brother and his wife from Waukegan, Illinois. I was excited to have them all be a part of the Graduation Review. It represented the climax of the story at Recruit Training Command. My family got to witness the results of all our hard work. The Review was held at Ross Field, and all 30 companies marched out onto the field one by one without the aid of the company commanders who had worked with us for nine long weeks. It was our chance to display newly-learned skills in military drill, military bearing, and to perform with the Navy's traditional pomp and ceremony. We had special units—the drum and bugle corps, the drill team, and the band. We stood at parade rest as the National Anthem was sung.

I will never forget that ceremony and the feeling of being a part of the United States Navy. I knew how much it meant to my family. One can see why military personnel get upset when civilian and professional athletes will not participate when the national anthem is played. I have corrected many young people over the years for their disrespect during the playing of the national anthem. I know firsthand a little about the sacrifices made by our nation's military veterans.

I am so grateful to God for the opportunity I had to serve my country. My Naval experience was so wonderful. I was given extra duties to help the other recruits in boot camp. Being older, and an Athletic Petty Office, I was able to assist with the fitness program. I did still have to go to happy hour with the other recruits.

After boot camp I was an administrative assistant to the company commanders at both the Naval Torpedo Station in Seattle, Washington, and the Navy Supply Depot in Charleston, South Carolina. While in Seattle, I played for the U.S. Navy. We played 44 regular season games, and I was privileged to be chosen to the All-Pacific Coast team. We played in the All-Navy Pacific Coast games in San Francisco. It pretty well sealed my desire to be a coach—that, coupled with my experiences with Coach Purcell.

JONESBORO GRADE SCHOOL 1969-1978

I finished my time in the United States Navy in April of 1969. In September, I began my first teaching job at Jonesboro Grade School. It really was neat that I would be teaching at the school I'd attended in the mid 1950s. The job paid $4,600, which was about $400 more than what I made in the U.S. Navy. A dollar went a lot farther in the '60s than it does now. I was blessed right away with an across the board raise of $600 taking my salary to $5,200—all before I'd taught one day of school. My new position included teaching junior high science, coaching basketball, baseball, and track, and serving as athletic director. The extra salary duties paid an additional $300, which came to 30 cents an hour! Coaching was a very long and consuming day.

COACHING AT JONESBORO

When I started at Jonesboro, like any teacher or coach, I had some long- and short-term goals. Success is what we all strive for. I also wanted to do well with the science program. My goal was to see my students gain a love for the environment and the natural world around them. We would participate in local science fairs as well as those at the regional and state levels. Being a competitive person, I wanted our students to learn, but I also wanted them to have an opportunity to compete at the regional and state level. The same thing would be true for our athletic teams. Later, this same concept would apply in my insurance career. Success was always my goal, and achieving goals requires hard work, focus, and dedication. Almost everyone can be successful, but the few who succeed in their endeavors do so because of two things—hard work and focus.

Sadly, we are becoming a society of entitlement. I have observed a division of people into 3%, 27%, & 70%. The 3%ers are the focused, hardworking, high-energy, and goal-driven people. The 27%ers are moderately successful and will do well because they understand the value of focus and investing some effort into goals, but they don't have the same energy level as the 3%ers. The 70%ers are the ones who fiddled their study halls away. They never learn how to work hard and pursue goals with passion.

We had some very successful years with our science and sports programs at Jonesboro. Our students bought into the values of goal-setting and hard work. We had those 3, 27, and 70%ers. Every business or school will have individuals who fit into these categories. However, it's the manager's or teacher's or coach's job to motivate their charges to be as successful as possible. A teacher or coach must push the right buttons to help each student or athlete understand the rewards of excellence. It's the winning spirit. Winning becomes a habit—a tradition.

Sadly, losing, or non-achievement can also become a habit and will become acceptable, if a person is not vigilant. I have seen this many times at all levels in my career.

In basketball at Jonesboro, Anna, and Anna-Jonesboro, our students learned how important it is to master the fundamentals. In order to excel in the fundamentals, they had to repeatedly practice skills. That required performing the drills over and over until they mastered them. I always said to them, "You must develop muscle memory, which means starting young and working hard over many years." Students have to stay focused, be willing to listen to the coach, and show up to practices.

In science, the same basic principles apply. Long hours must be spent on facts, attitude, commitment, a competitive spirit and the desire to improve. Paula and I attended a Peter Lowe seminar in the early '90s. Zig Ziglar was one of the speakers, along with Charlton Heston, who played Moses in the 1956 epic *The Ten Commandments*. It was an amazing experience for the two of us. Mr. Ziglar stressed the need to understand that the path from where you are to where you want to be is not always smooth and straight. The reason for the twists and bumps is simple, and it has nothing to do with you. It has more to do with the fact that not everyone is as interested in your success as you are. Some people may accidentally hinder your efforts; others, who are in competition with you and have little integrity, may even try to sabotage your efforts. Charlton Heston was asked, "How hard was it to learn the dozens and dozens of pages of script?" Mr. Heston replied, "It took hours and hours of hard work." But that day, Mr. Heston was still able to perform several lines from the movie. It was awesome!

PHYSICAL FITNESS

The Navy physical fitness program helped me years later when I coached and taught physical education. It was quite an apprenticeship program. Navy boot camp was very tough. I kid my good friend Ron Hinkle about how easy Air Force boot camp was, compared to mine. He agreed up to a point. We did hundreds of push-ups and sit-ups. If one person messed up in marching or going through the 96-count Manual-of-Arms, all 90 of us had to report to the armory for "Happy Hour." We thought, "Wow, 'Happy Hour'! That sounds nice." During my first years at Lick Creek, the kids thought the same thing at first, "How nice for the coach to give us a 'happy hour'." They found out soon enough that it was not what they expected. The Navy happy hour was one full hour

My last day in the United States Navy, 1969

of calisthenics. We did push-ups, sit-ups, planks, jumping jacks, sprints, and stretching. My happy hour at Lick Creek is only 40 minutes of the same calisthenics. (I didn't have to introduce the happy hour at Jonesboro Grade school, right after my Navy duty. I didn't need it, because we still had the board of education (the paddle), but it disappeared in 1976.)

MY INSURANCE CAREER

Early in my teaching and coaching career, I was approached by two of my friends who were insurance agents. I was having baseball practice at the Jonesboro Grade School. It was late April, and I was taking infield with the team. Darryl Ury and Gary Buckner drove over to the field. They wanted me to come to Ury Insurance Agency on the square when practice was over. In fact, they loaded me in their pickup and drove me to the agency. I think they thought I might not show up.

They offered me an opportunity during the summer months to sell individual health policies for Principal Mutual Life Insurance Company. The company was out of Des Moines, Iowa, and the marketing firm was Rogers Benefit Group, home-based in Minneapolis, Minnesota.

My first reaction was, "Guys, I'm a coach. I'm not interested in selling insurance policies." They assured me it would be for the summer only. "We are having a contest with another insurance firm in Missouri." Another agency near St. Louis is offering the same opportunity to a teacher in that area. Two of the general agents at Rogers Benefit Group made a bet on which teacher could sell the most policies. I reluctantly agreed to try. They offered me $600 a month for three months. That was very good money for 1979. The deal still stood, whether I sold a policy or not. My competitive nature and work ethic made me want to sell as many health insurance policies as I could. I wasn't licensed, so Gary Buckner would sign all my applications and act as my supervisor.

I began right away to study the products I would be marketing. I wasn't at all sure that I would be a good enough salesman to even consider an insurance career. I was very pleased to be teaching and coaching. However, my pay was very poor for all the duties I had at the school. I was the science teacher for four classes of seventh and eighth graders, as well as the health and physical education teacher. My extracurricular activities included serving as basketball, baseball, and track coach and yearbook advisor. I figured my pay was less than three dollars an hour.

The school year ended in late May, and I began my summer job in early June. My competitive spirit inspired me to outsell that teacher in the St. Louis area. I knew many people in the Union County area as I had grown up there, and I had met many more people through my work with kids for almost ten years. I made a list of many friends and acquaintances and began making calls. In 1979, insurance was not nearly as expensive as it is today. A plan that could cover an entire medical bill cost only about $80 a month. For an annual cost of less $1,000, a person could insure his whole family. Room and board ran about $110 a day or less back then. Now, in 2019, we often see rates of $2,000 a month for a family. Drug prices have soared to levels unheard of in 1979. We are currently facing a crisis with the high cost of drugs.

After gathering a significant number of contacts, I devised a plan. I knew, through coaching, that to have a good team one must teach the fundamentals over and over. The drills would have to be done many times to develop skill. I knew that I would need to make many phone calls. Many agents fail because they have "call reluctance" or a poor work ethic. Insurance, like a lot of marketing, is a numbers game. We have all received junk mail. We think, "Why would they send me this mail? They should know I'm not interested in their product." But it works for marketing companies because they send out thousands of letters. They may only get a return of 3 or 4%. But the mailing expense is minimal compared to all of the products they sell. It's a numbers game. I understood this concept and would make dozens of calls each day to try and set up sit-down appointments.

I was able to sell 33 individual polices and land a couple of employer groups that first summer. The amount of sales totalled approximately $40,000.

The Rogers Benefit Firm in St. Louis was thrilled with that amount. The agent whom I'd competed with fizzled out in the first month, selling only a few policies. I was offered a full-time job with the general agency, located in Chesterfield, Missouri, near St. Louis, but I had signed a contract to teach at Anna-Jonesboro Community High School. I was always taught that if you sign a contract, you must honor the commitment. I called the company and said that I had signed a contract to teach at AJ. By then, it was late August, and school was about to start.

I wasn't convinced I wanted to leave a job I enjoyed. My pay had already increased from $12,000 to $18,000—a very large sum for the late '70s. I would be taking a risk selling insurance, and the area I would be assigned would be southern Illinois, western Kentucky, southern Indiana, and southeast Missouri—a large territory. My job would be as a general agent, which meant I would have to recruit and train local agents. I would be considered a wholesaler and would be paid a fee from the sales of the agents I recruited.

School started, and three weeks later I was sitting in a faculty meeting at Anna-Jonesboro Community High School. Other than the first staff meeting at the start of school, this was my first one at AJ. However, this meeting was held to vote on whether or not to strike. I must have been naïve about what was going on, because I wasn't expecting my second faculty meeting to be a vote on a teacher strike. The majority voted to strike. (It was the first and only one in school history.) I was saddened and very uncomfortable because many of the students I had taught at Jonesboro Grade School were angry with me. I always tried to put the interest of the students first, and I didn't believe we, as a staff, had done that.

I've forgotten many of the details surrounding that time, but I do remember that a couple of coaches almost got into a fight. One was in favor of it, and the other opposed it because it meant that games would have to be forfeited. Thankfully, the strike didn't last long, but I witnessed a divided staff and some unprofessional attitudes. I started thinking the insurance position might be a good idea for me. Maybe I was ready for a new challenge.

Because of the strike, my contract was invalidated. I immediately typed up my resignation letter and submitted it to the superintendent. He lost no time in accepting my resignation. The strike meant the school district would need more money to pay the teachers. My $18,000 salary went back into the budget, and my position wasn't filled but absorbed by the other teachers.

I became the shortest-tenured teacher in the history of the school. I have always "blamed" two students for driving me out of teaching—Jeff Starr and Kendra Moore (Edwards)whom I'd had in physical science. Jeff had just appeared in the movie *Bad News Bears* and was feeling his oats. Kendra was basically just a cut-up. I still accuse them of running me out of teaching. Kendra is a teacher herself now, and both are very good friends of mine with successful careers of their own.

I contacted Mr. Dick Schubbe, the Regional Manager, and he got me started with the different insurance courses I would have to study for my insurance license. I spent September and October preparing for the insurance examination. My home would be my office until I got my business built. I lived right across from the old ball field. The hardest thing for me was watching the Jonesboro kids playing on the playground and my former teams practicing. I wondered if I would be happy with the career change. It was gut-wrenching at first, but I couldn't go back, I had to move on.

I passed the test in late October and started working for Rogers Benefit Group out of the Chesterfield office. I spent much of November training and working with Mr. Schubbe. I had to meet with the CEO of the firm in Minneapolis, Minnesota, a little later. I was nervous. The interview started with the president, Marv Siebold, telling me that the job would be very similar to choosing a basketball team. He knew that I had coached a number of years. He told me some agents would be successful, and others would not make the team. I don't know what came over me, but I asked, "Yes, but will the angry mothers call me when I cut their kids off the team?" He erupted with laughter. Rapport was established, and we had a great interview. He seemed comfortable enough to say, "Let's give this young coach a try." Mr. Siebold secured the approval of Mr. Pat Rogers, the CEO and founder of the marketing company. Pat was a former University of Notre Dame lineman. I sure enjoyed sitting down with him one-on-one to talk sports and insurance over my years with company.

The stage was set for me to start soliciting and training agents. It was a tremendous challenge and so much different than my teaching career. I had taught and coached at Jonesboro Grade School for ten years. I did miss the kids, and I often look back and wonder what I would have done if I hadn't gotten past the interview. I must have had plenty of faith. I'm sure Mr. Dick Schubbe's positive comments about my accomplishment during the summer was taken into account.

The time came to begin a series of meetings with potential insurance reps to sell our policies. There were many independent insurance and life insurance agencies in the four-state area. It would require making calls and getting appointments set up to discuss our product. I realized that those agents were already very knowledgeable in their product line. However, many didn't concentrate in the area of health, so that could be an avenue for them to increase their sales base. My job would be to sell why our product was worthy of marketing. I had to emphasize customer service, our company track record over the years, our A-plus rating, our rates, and our coverage. One thing that our competition didn't have was that our policies had an unlimited lifetime maximum on them. Most companies had only a million-dollar maximum. That was huge, due to the rising cost of hospital and medical coverage. One element that caused healthcare to rise was the cost to doctors for medical malpractice insurance. Also, people in our society are more likely to file claims than in the past—mainly because of the high cost of their losses. It is an appropriate action if a loved one suffers or even dies because of a mistake made by a surgeon or the misuse of a drug.

Dick Schubbe and I began to work the two states of Illinois and Missouri; Indiana and Kentucky would be added later. I needed to find five agents and eventually build a team of fifteen. Our meetings in Carbondale and Cape Girardeau would include 12-15 agents each. We wanted to keep the groups small and personal. Sometimes we would have more and sometimes less. Of course, after getting agents signed, we had to train them before they could sell our product. Over my twelve years we signed approximately 100 agents. Many didn't make the team. As with a ball team, they didn't have the work ethic, skill, and commitment needed. The 3%, 27%, and 70% rule applied. Occasionally, some of the 70%ers who didn't apply themselves in school realize later in life that they need to get their act together. They can become 27%ers or even 3%ers.

Over the years, our top agencies were the Northwestern Mutual agencies. They were very personable and also very professional. Those people were all 3%ers, and the company is one of the largest life insurance companies in the world. Since those agents had many clients with life insurance only, we were able to offer them a product for personal health coverage. My job was to assist them with the presentations for both individual health and group health. One big advantage that I had was that I could field underwrite and approve their groups plans. It was very important that I thoroughly check each group for any health issues. A mistake in underwriting the plan could bring on the wrath of my home office bosses. In order to remain competitive, we had to hold claims in check. The sales had to be made, or I wouldn't make the team. There was a lot of pressure on me in the very beginning. I had to sell myself on why I should be their agent. Service was the key. Pat Rogers always said, "We pay you commissions, and that is for servicing the products."

I had Northwestern Mutual agencies in Carbondale, IL; Herrin, IL; Cape Girardeau, MO; Sikeston, MO; Paducah, KY; and Madisonville, KY. Those agencies had approximately 120 small employer group health plans and about 230 individual policies written through our agency over twelve years. Up until five years ago, I was still receiving commissions on the business written by those agents and independent agencies as far back as 1980. Much of the business was still on the books long after my retirement in 1991. Retention and service are the ultimate keys to success in the insurance business. I was allowed to retire with half of my commissions for as long as the business stayed on the books. I was still receiving commissions in 2014. The nice part about it was that I received commissions without having to do any service work. It was a very nice retirement package offered by the company.

I'm very proud of those agents and agencies after all these years. Like so many of my kids at Jonesboro Grade

School and Lick Creek, they did what it took to be winners. There is no substitute for work ethic and relationships.

Upon my retirement in 1991, our agents had written 1,000 groups and about 1,200 individual policies. I wanted to work longer with Rogers Benefit Group, but they decided to combine all the rural agencies into the metropolitan offices. I thought it was a bad idea. Our rural agency was producing a million dollars a year in the four-state area. The relationships were already established. I called John Rogers, the son of founder Pat Rogers, and told him I would not be willing to move to St. Louis. The company took my block of business and would service it. I found out a few years later that the St. Louis office was merged with the Springfield, Missouri, office. Closing the rural markets down proved to be a bad move. The metropolitan agents didn't have the rapport with the local agents that the rural general agents had had. My decision to not go to St. Louis turned out to be the right one. It wasn't long before I received a call from Edward M. Smith to be his health benefit manager for the Laborers' International Union of North America. I would work out of the health and welfare fund in Cairo, Illinois. The Lord continued to bless me in that career change.

FINAL THOUGHTS

- Be proactive by taking charge of your own life. Act in a positive and beneficial way rather than reacting to things that you have no control over. I still battle with this myself quite often. When I'm aware of it, I step back and reevaluate the situation. I tell myself,

181

"I have no control over what just happened, so act in a positive way."

- Refuse to settle for a future controlled by others or by chance. If we are not careful, we let someone else control what our future will be. Many times, parents want a certain thing for their child, however the child wants to go in a different direction. We must follow our passion and desire. Many people are living a life they didn't choose for themselves. That is very sad. A lifetime is a long time to do something that was chosen by someone else.

- Become the master of your life and not the victim. Bob Love could have been the victim, but he chose to be the master, overcoming the disability of stuttering and the disadvantage of growing up in poverty. He became an NBA All-Star for the Chicago Bulls. Even more impressively, he received speech therapy and now speaks to thousands of people across the country as a spokesperson and Director of Community Affairs for the Bulls. With the right attitude in life, anyone can achieve success.

In my studies, and in my careers as coach, Navy officer, insurance agent, and health and safety director for the Laborers' organization, I have observed people who are consciously thinking what direction they want their life to move, and they have taken steps to make it happen. I've been impressed by so many of my former athletes who have gone on to become All-State or All-American. One young man even made the 1996 Olympic team in high jump. Many students have chosen careers in which they have become very successful. Many have become doctors, attorneys, nurses, and teachers, to name a few. That didn't just happen. They planned their life goals, including personal relationships, personal growth, and physical and mental fitness. All of these attributes are part of the path to success. They refused to be victims. They found their passion, and they pursued it.

A FEW MORE HELPFUL QUOTES

Without goals you become what you were.
With goals, you become what you wish.
                                    — Anonymous

We can't do anything about the wind; we
can only adjust the sails.
                                    — Anonymous

If you can dream it, you can become it. If
you can imagine it, you can achieve it.
                                    — Unknown

Positive is better. You resemble the
thought which you conceive.
                                    — Goethe

I only pass through this life once.
Therefore, if there is any kindness I can
give you, let me do so now, for I may not
pass this way again.
                                    — Gale Sayers

It is one of the most beautiful
compensations of this life that no man
can seriously help another without helping
himself.
> — Ralph Waldo Emerson

Be happy all life - some sun, some rain.
> — R. Kirsten-Daiensai

Most people are just about as happy as
they decide to be.
> — Abraham Lincoln

Wisdom comes more from understanding
than from knowledge.
> — Anonymous

Each of us exists to carry out a special
mission a task that belongs to no other.
> — R. Kirsten-Daiensai

We are what we repeatedly do. Excellence,
then, is not an act but a habit.
> — Anonymous

It is not the things around us which
matter, but our attitude toward things.
> — Marcus Aurelius

Life is what we make it; always has been,
always will be.

— Grandma Moses

Behold the turtle. He makes progress only
when he sticks his neck out.

— Anonymous

Whatever you can do or dream, you can,
begin it. Boldness has genius, power, and
magic in it. BEGIN IT NOW.

— Goethe

There is no such thing as too many hugs.

— R. Kirsten-Daiensai

Good friendships are fragile things and
require as much care as other fragile and
precious things.

— Randolph Bourne

The most important thing in life is to learn
how to give out love, and to let it come in.

— Mitch Albom

Myself with U.S. Olympic High Jumper Cameron Wright (1996) at our Laborers' meeting in Springfield, Illinois

From left: Jake Parr, Zach Parr (holding the 2nd place trophy), Logan Mattingly, and Hunter Garver

David Excstein, STL Cardinals World Series MVP 2005 with my grandson Reid Zellner in Memphis. Reid lived next door to David's inlaws.

Lick Creek 3rd place state girl's track team.

Me with my VBS kids at Gilead Church in Simpson, IL.